Experiences in Bhakti:

the Science Celestial

Experiences in Bhakti: the Science Celestial

O. B. L. Kapoor
(Ādikeśava Dāsa)

Fourth (Golden Avatar) Edition

Edited, annotated, and introduced
by
Neal Delmonico

Golden Avatar Press
715 E. McPherson
Kirksville, Missouri 63501
2014

First Edition: 1994
Second Edition: 2006
Third (Paperback) Editon: 2012
Fourth (Golden Avatar) Edition: 2014

ISBN 978-1-936135-05-9 (1-936135-05-1) (Paperback)

Library of Congress Control Number: 2014944660

Published by:
Golden Avatar Press
715 E. McPherson
Kirksville, Missouri 63501

Available at:
Nitai's Bookstore
715 E. McPherson
Kirksville, Missouri, 63501
Phone: (660) 665-0273
http://www.nitaisbookstore.com
http://www.blazing-sapphire-press.com
Email: neal@blazing-sapphire-press.com

Image Credits

Image on Front Cover:
Attributed to: The Family of Nainsukh
Krishna and His Favorite Shelter from a Storm (detail)
Indian, Pahari, about 1825
Opaque watercolor and gold on paper
Overall: 29.7 x 21.1 cm (11 11/16 x 8 5/16 in.)
Other (Image only): 16.7 x 24.5 cm (6 5/8 x 9 5/8 in.)
Museum of Fine Arts, Boston
Ross-Coomaraswamy Collection, 17.2614
Museum of Fine Arts, Boston
Ross-Coomaraswamy Collection
Photograph ©Museum of Fine Arts, Boston

Image on Back Cover:
Krishna Fluting for Gopas and Cows (detail)
Indian, Pahari, about 1700
Opaque watercolor and silver on paper
Overall: 16 x 24.5 cm (6 5/16 x 9 5/8 in.)
Museum of Fine Arts, Boston
Ross-Coomaraswamy Collection, 17.2804

Museum of Fine Arts, Boston
Ross-Coomaraswamy Collection
Photograph ©Museum of Fine Arts, Boston

Contents

Publisher's Preface (Third Edition) ix

Editor's Preface (Third Edition) xiii

Chapter One: What is *Bhakti*? 3
Bhakti, a Function of the *Hlādinī-śakti* 3
Bhakti, the Selfless, Loving Service of Bhagavān 4
Bhakti, a Spiritual Gravitational Force 5
Bhakti, the Only Way to Attain Bhagavān 6
Bhakti, the Essence of All Religions 7

Chapter Two: Is *Bhakti* a Science? 11
Bhakti is Science in a Higher Sense 11
Bhakti Properly Called a Science 12
Bhakti Alone Acquires Knowledge of God 13
Bhakti Alone Purifies the Understanding and Senses 17
The Laws of the Science of *Bhakti* Alone are Certain 18

Chapter Three: The Laws of *Bhakti* 23
The Law of Gravitation 23
Examples 25
Bāla-gopāla served by Kṛṣṇa Prema 25
Śrī Kṛṣṇa Candramā served by Lālā Bābu 26
Gaura and Nitāi Served by Pisi Mā Gosvāminī (Candraśaśī) 26
The Law of Reciprocation 27
The Law of Subjugation 31
The Law of Unification 34

Chapter Four: Are the Laws of the Science of *Bhakti* Verifiable? 39
The Laws of *Bhakti* Do Not Need Verification Because They Are Based on Revelation 39
The Validity of Revelation is Vindicated by Modern Science . . 40
Though Not Needed, the Laws of *Bhakti* Can Be Verified 41

Chapter Five: Verification of the Law of Gravitation 45
Bhakti in the Hearts of the Devotees 45
Examples 46
Lokanātha Gosvāmin and Ṭhākura Rādhāvinoda 46
Sanātana Gosvāmin and Ṭhākura Madanagopāla 47
Gaurāṅga Dāsa Bābā and Girirāja 49
Jaikṛṣṇa Dāsa Bābā and Śrī Kṛṣṇa 50
Gauracaraṇa Dāsa Bābā and Dāujī (Balarāma) 52
Śrī Rādhāramaṇacaraṇa Dāsa Deva 53
Kṛṣṇa Attracted by Offerings 56
Examples 57
The Khīr of Pisi Mā Gosvāminī 57
Ṭhākura Madanamohana and the Gūjarī's Milk 58
Lord Jagannātha and the Khicuri of Karamā Bāi 61
Govindadeva and the Gardener's Pomegranate 64
Kṛṣṇa Attracted by Dance, *Kīrtana* and Talks 66
Examples 67
The Song of the Cowherd Girls and Śrī Kṛṣṇa 67
Stories about Kṛṣṇa 68
Recitation of the *Bhāgavata* 70
The *Saṅkīrtana* of Ṭhākura Candra Sinha 72
The *Saṅkīrtana* of Harisevakajī 73

Chapter Six: Verification of the Law of Reciprocation 75
Examples 75
Ṭhākura and Dhannā Jāta 75
Gopāla and Kṛṣṇaprema (Ronald Nixon) 80
Gopīnātha and Govinda Ghoṣa 81
Gopāla and Durgī Mā 84
Raṅganātha and Āṇḍāla 87
Giridhara Gopāla and Mīrā 89
Śrī Viśvanātha Cakravartin and the Mañjarī Identity . . . 94
Sacred Images and the Feelings of the *Bhakta* 96

Chapter Seven: Verification of the Law of Subjugation 99
Examples 99
Bhagavān as Barber Sena and Rāja Vīrasiṃha 99
Bhagavān as Parasarāma Khātī and Rāja Jayamala 100
Bhagavān as Boatman and Sanehī Rāma 102
Bhagavān as Servant in the Temple of Madanamohana and Tāja Khān 103
Bhagavān as Demonstrator at Mahārāja's College, Jaipur, and Mādho Lāla Māthura 107

Chapter Eight: Verification of the Law of Unification 111
Examples 112
Kṛṣṇa Himself Fought a War for Rāja Jayamala Rāṭhora . 112
Girirāja Himself Brought Grace-food for Lālā Bābu 115
Rādhā Brought Food for Madhusūdana Dāsa Bābājī 116
Kṛṣṇa Pays Revenue for Kiśana Sinha Rāṭhora 118
Rādhā Restored the Eyes of the Blind Bābā of Madanaṭera 122
Lord Jagannātha Lied to Save Jagadbandhu Mahāpātra . 124
Lord Jagannātha Rendered Menial Service to Mādhava Dāsa Bābā 128
Rādhā and Kṛṣṇa Massaged Mā Maṇi 133

The Author 137

Other Books by Golden Avatar Press 139
Coming soon: 139
And From Blazing Sapphire Press 139
Coming soon from Blazing Sapphire: 143

Publisher's Preface (Third Edition)

Thank you God, Guru, and Vaiṣṇavas for the opportunity to write a few words about this fine book, written by a dear friend and mentor. I was fortunate to have spent a great deal of time with Dr. Kapoor during the late 1970s and 1980s. After several years of friendship, he invited me to stay in an upper room of his house and thus I lived with him for many months.

We talked then about my translating his Hindi books into English for a Western audience. When I later realized my lack of commitment to spending the time necessary to master the language, I pleaded with him to translate them into English himself. I later found out that several years after my stay with him he had done exactly that. I thank him from the depths of my heart.

The book republished here is one of my favorite books by Dr. Kapoor, and since it is now only available in an expensive hardbound edition, Nitai Das and I wanted to see it published in a less expensive paperback format. We undertook the republication of this work with the permission and encouragement of Dr. Kapoor's son Gopesh Kapoor.

The republication of this fine work is ninety-nine percent the work of Nitai Das who painstakingly typed the whole book into the computer and then carefully edited the work into its current state. I spent only a small amount of time proofreading, giving suggestions here and there to smooth out a few rough sentences. So congratulations and great thanks go to him.

Dr. Kapoor was a great *bhakta* (devotee). He was instrumental in introducing me to many of the great *bhakta-sādhus* (devotee saints) of his own illustrious lineage, that of Śrī Rādhāramaṇ Caraṇ Dāss Dev. It was a wonderful time for me, a time filled with great blessings!

In reading this book, I hope you will find understanding and faith, and the inspiration to follow the path of selfless, loving devotion to Bhagavān (God). It is my sincere wish that we all reap the fruit of *bhagavat-prema* (divine love of God), taste it and nourish our lives by it—and in so doing become great examples of saintliness ourselves.

I feel it needs mentioning that each of the many hundreds, if not thousands, of *bhaktas* who has achieved success (*siddhi*) in having direct, loving, intimate interactions with the original source God (*svayam bhagavān*) on a regular basis has reached that goal after many years of diligent and committed practice on the path. Although some seem like they suffer greatly from the torments of separation after first seeing and interacting with Bhagavān and then finding themselves bereft of his presence–this pain of separation is actually filled with a special kind of sustaining, divine energy flowing from Bhagavān. Thus, the suffering experienced is of a transcendent nature and expands the capacity of the *bhakta*'s heart to accommodate greater and greater divine love. This makes the *bhakta* ever more sweet and desireable for Svayam Bhagavān, Śrī Kṛṣṇa, and their interactions become ever more pleasurable for him as well. One can imagine that as one continues in this way to enlarge and further intensify the elation of love-in-absence, the eventual reunion becomes astonishingly joyful, and beyond that another cycle of rarified growth begins.

Another thing worth mentioning is the importance of the long-term cultivation of a true and deeply penetrating selflessness with regard to one's loving devotion to God. This may look to outsiders like timidity, but it is in fact an authentic humility. Humility arises through beholding pure, illuminated divinity in a variety of ways and must assuredly include ever deepening, ever active, direct loving interactions with that divinity. We can read between the lines of the revealed personal accounts and experiences of some saints and realize that the amount and variety of interactions between saint and Bhagavān Śrī Kṛṣṇa which occur on a daily basis must be prolific, far-reaching and brilliant. Such interactions are not normally revealed and, if they were, they would not in all likelihood be correctly understood. True understanding of such indescribable experiences is accumulated through years of committed practice.

In closing, I want to dedicate sincerely any merit this effort might generate to Dr. Kapoor himself—a great man and *sādhu*, a dear friend of my heart—to his illustrious lineage of gurus—starting with his own blessed *gurudev*, Śrī Śrī 108 Gaurāṅga Dās Bābājī, his *parama guru*, Śrī Śrī 108 Rām Dās Bābājī Mahārāj, his *parameṣṭhī guru*, Śrī Śrī 1008 Rādhāramaṇ Caraṇ Dās Dev—and to all people who want to attain, with clarity and depth, selfless loving devotion to God and Guru.

Jay Śrī Guru-Vaiṣṇav!

Jagadish Dass
Kirksville, Missouri
November 11, 2011

Editor's Preface (Third Edition)

Dr. O. B. L. Kapoor was a brilliant man and a great devotee of Kṛṣṇa. His earlier book, *The Philosophy and Religion of Śrī Caitanya*, has now become a classic, respected and studied by devotee and scholar alike. In that one volume, one could say, he accomplished more than others have in fifty. Though he was a devout Vaiṣṇava, he had the trained mind and sensitivity of a philosopher and a scholar, and thus he had a highly developed ability to think logically and deeply about things. Certainly, his remarks about Śrī Caitanya, in the preface of the aforementioned book, apply equally well to Dr. Kapoor:

> It is a mistake to suppose that the predominance of emotions in the life of a devotee renders him incapable of serious philosophical thinking. On the contrary, his understanding is so developed and purified that his grasp of things is more intuitive than ratiocinative and his knowledge of reality is more intimate and complete. His emotions are the natural outcome of his close apprehension of Reality.[1]

While I am not sure how far many of us are willing to go in considering the devotee's knowledge to be "more intimate and complete,"[2] one can concede that experiencing powerful, religious emotions does not necessarily disqualify one from thinking well philosophically. Dr.

[1] Kapoor, *The Philosophy and Religion of Śrī Caitanya*, "Preface," p. xi.

[2] Knowing the maker intimately does not necessarily entail intimate knowledge of what the maker has made. Both might remain essentially beyond the knowing capacity of the knower.

Kapoor's ability to think well philosophically is what makes his work such a pleasure to read and also such a great source of edification and understanding. His books have a breadth and richness to them that is usually missing in works written to support a particular religious tradition, especially a tradition that foregrounds emotion. As in the present work, in which he cites the words and thoughts of several great twentieth century scientists, Kapoor often refers to the ideas of great thinkers of both the East and the West. This practice serves to bring Caitanya Vaiṣṇavism out of its shell and into the arena of world philosophical and religious discourse where it surely belongs. Moreover, his clear and insightful presentation of the ideas and practices of the Caitanya tradition makes them easily understandable to twenty-first century readers from a variety of cultures, religious traditions, and world views. This, too, he commented on in the preface to his *Philosophy and Religion of Śrī Caitanya*:

> It is not necessary for a devotee, who is in direct and intimate touch with reality, to supplement his knowledge by undergoing training in one of the accredited schools of learning. But Śrī Caitanya had the additional advantage of high scholarship, which enabled him to express his thoughts with the precision, accuracy, and consistency that characterizes a system of philosophy.[3]

There is an intimate connection between the ability to express oneself and the ability to think. It is in this, surely, that Dr. Kapoor excels.

Apart from the classic work mentioned above, Dr. Kapoor has written many other books in English and his native language, Hindi. I will not list them all here. A complete list of his English works can be found in the bibliography. Some of his books are still available from various sources, but many are now out of print and hard to come by. It is, therefore, a great pleasure for us at Blazing Sapphire Press to announce that we are working with Dr. Kapoor's son Śrī Gopesh Kapoor to bring back into publication all the books of the good doctor that have gone out of print. While Śrī Gopesh Kapoor is busily engaged in having the Hindi works of his father reprinted in India, we are re-editing and re-issuing his major works in English here in the USA and Europe. This volume is

[3] ibid.

the first result of those efforts. Other volumes now out of print are currently being worked on and will be available in the future. Moreover, as copies of the older editions are exhausted, they, too, will be taken up for republication. Eventually we hope to have the whole corpus of Dr. Kapoor's works available in fine editions here and around the world. Śrī Gopesh informs me that this was one of his father's greatest wishes and deepest concerns during his last days here on earth.

On a more personal note Dr. Kapoor was a dear friend and a mentor of mine many long years ago. He was then a healthy man in his 60s, recently retired from a distinguished career of teaching philosophy at several colleges and his final position as the principal of the Government College at Gyanpur/Rampur near Varanasi in Uttar Pradesh. I lived in Vrindaban for a year or two back in the mid-1970s, and I used to visit him in the afternoons when I had some spare time. His timely intervention resulted in a profound change in the direction of my life, one which I have never had cause to regret.

We would sit in his parlor talking for hours about all aspects of Caitanya Vaiṣṇavism and about his experiences as a practicing member of the tradition. He told me how he had started out as a young philosopher who embraced the non-dualist (Advaita) philosophical position of Vedānta and had seen that philosophy profoundly critiqued during a series of lectures by the Vaiṣṇava teacher, Bhaktisiddhānta Sarasvatī, in the 1930s. After that, he became a disciple of that Vaiṣṇava savant and took up the study and practice of Caitanya Vaiṣṇavism. It was later, in the 1960s, I believe, that Kapoor and his wife met the great Vaiṣṇava saint[4] Śrī Gaurāṅga Dāsa Bābā, a disciple of the saint Rāma Dāsa Bābā (1876-1953) of the *Nitāi Gaura Rādhā Śyām* tradition.[5] Dr. Kapoor told me that as soon as they met the saint, he and his wife were overcome with powerful religious emotions and knew that he was the spiritual guide they had been waiting for. They became his disciples and visited him often at his *āśrama* on Ramanreti road in Vrindaban.

Every time we were together he would be busy reciting the names of Kṛṣṇa under his breath and moving a string of beads in a small bag

---

[4]Saint in this context means a *bhakta* or member of the Caitanya tradition who is believed to have achieved the highest goal of the practice, a direct vision of and continued intimacy with Śrī Kṛṣṇa and Śrīmatī Rādhikā.

[5]This is a relatively modern movement or sub-sect of the Caitanya tradition that was founded in the 19th century by the saint Śrī Rādhāramaṇa Caraṇa Deva Dāsa Bābā (1853-1905).

to keep count of his recitations. He told me that his guru, Śrī Gaurāṅga Dāsa Bābā, and the tradition of Caitanya Vaiṣṇavism to which he belonged recommended such constant and counted chanting. Also, unless I am mistaken, we discussed during that period many of the ideas found in this book. I believe he was in the process of writing it at the time, though it was not published until nearly twenty years later. That personal connection with the book is certainly one of the reasons I am so pleased to be able to present a new edition of *Experiences in Bhakti*, a book that is arguably among his finest.

This book is about *bhakti*, a difficult term and concept to translate into a non-Indic language. It is often translated as "devotion" in English and it does bear a similarity to that idea and to the idea of "piety." But, *bhakti* carries with it a lot more than is found in either of the ideas of devotion or piety. For example, it contains the idea of relationship between a devotee and whatever being that devotee recognizes as god. Therefore, Dr. Kapoor chose to leave *bhakti* largely untranslated in this book and I have continued that practice. The whole book is in fact an effort to elucidate or unpack the idea of *bhakti*.

Dr. Kapoor provided a useful overview of his work in his preface to the first edition:

> In the first chapter of the book the transcendental character of *bhakti* has been explained and it has been emphasized that *bhakti* is an essential part of every religious discipline that leads to God. In the second an attempt has been made to prove that *bhakti* alone is a science in the real sense of the term. Modern science has already ceased to lay claim to any knowledge of the Truth or the Ultimate Reality as such. It disbelieves in the very existence of matter, which nineteenth century scientists regarded as the ultimate reality. Its discoveries necessarily point to the existence of a conscious being behind what is called matter, which, it is humble enough to confess, it cannot know. It also confesses that its laws are not certain, but only probable to the extent that they make life possible.
>
> The third chapter enunciates and explains the four fundamental laws of *bhakti*. The fourth states that the laws of *bhakti* do not stand in need of verification because they are of divine origin, but stresses that they are experimentally

> verifiable like the laws of any other science.
>
> The last four chapters show how the laws of *bhakti* already stand verified by the experiences of the saints. One chapter is devoted to each law and numerous experiences from the lives of the saints have been adduced to prove it.
>
> The experiences have been carefully selected from a wide range of biographical literature pertaining to the saints who pursued the path of pure *bhakti*. They reveal the inner workings of the spiritual world of *bhakti* and inspire fresh hope and confidence in the hearts of people who have lost their way in the maze of *māyā* and stand badly in need of light and guidance.[6]

Thus, the early chapters place *bhakti* in a broader context, comparing it to modern science and placing it in the context of what we now call the History of Religions. In the later chapters, Dr. Kapoor organizes a plethora of Vaiṣṇava stories which illustrate *bhakti* as it is known in Caitanya Vaiṣṇavism, a tradition which identifies the supreme being as Kṛṣṇa.

What is *bhakti*, then? *Bhakti* is primarily a state of mind (*mano-vṛtti*). To ordinary people it may even seem like a mad state of mind. Speaking to stone or metal images or to ethereal beings who cannot be seen by others, sometimes crying profusely, sometimes trembling violently, sometimes collapsing in faints, sometimes shouting out loudly and laughing: these are some of the products of the *bhakti* state of mind. The stories Dr. Kapoor has gathered to demonstrate his four principles of *bhakti* are filled with such things. Theologically speaking, Caitanya Vaiṣṇavas believe *bhakti* to be the presence in a person's mind of an aspect of one of Kṛṣṇa's divine powers, called the *hlādinī-śakti*, the pleasure-giving power. Its presence in the mind of a person makes him or her a source of great pleasure for Kṛṣṇa and coincidentally gives that person great pleasure as well, causing that person to feel intense attraction for Kṛṣṇa and often to behave in the ways described above. Jīva Gosvāmin says:

> The force called the pleasure-giving power (*hlādinī-śakti*) is the essential core of the internal power (*svarūpa-śakti*) [of

[6] Kapoor, *Experiences in Bhakti: the Science Celestial*, First Edition, Preface, xi-xii.

> Kṛṣṇa] which is itself the most essential of all of the Lord's powers. In turn, the essential core of that pleasure power is the special operation (*vṛtti*, faculty?) *bhakti* and is also known as attraction (*rati*)."[7]

The pleasure-giving power is not considered to be a natural product. Śrī Rūpa Gosvāmin describes it as a special kind of pure existence or being (*śuddha-sattva-viśeṣātman*).[8] It is believed to come from outside of the natural world, to descend into the mind of a person and to fill it like a powerful intoxicating fragrance.[9] That fragrance, it so happens, is irresistible to Kṛṣṇa who is drawn to it like a bee to a flower in bloom. That power, therefore, is a supernatural power. Those into whom it descends become like persons possessed, and that, to some degree, explains the many similarities between some of the manifestations of *bhakti* and madness.

Dr. Kapoor's dozens of carefully selected and sweetly told stories illustrate the variety of *bhakti* experiences of some of the saints in his tradition and in other closely related traditions, as various hagiographical texts record them. Because Dr. Kapoor was a fine rhetorician as well as a walking encyclopedia of Vaiṣṇava stories, his presentation is attractive, carefully organized, and (to the right audience) persuasive. But is *bhakti* a science? Because this is one of the major directions Dr. Kapoor's argument takes in this book, it is worth looking at it more closely in the context of religious studies generally.

Bhakti certainly may play an important role in scientific endeavors. For instance, it has an important part to play in the scientific or academic study of religion, as do numerous other religious phenomena from around the world. One major methodology of the academic study of religion is called the History of Religions, a discipline that has its roots in the earlier European study of religion called in German *Religionswissenschaft.* According to Cassell's German dictionary, *wissenschaft* means "science or knowledge." So the word *religionswissenschaft* means the "science of religions." This is, of course, an older usage of the word "science" in which it means a field or an area of study, a body of knowl-

---

[7] Jīva Gosvāmin, *Paramātma-sandarbha*, para 92 [my translation]: *kiṃca paramasārabhūtāyā api svarūpaśakteḥ sārabhūtā hlādinī nāma yā vṛttistasyā eva sārabhūto vṛttiviśeṣo bhaktiḥ sā ca ratyaparaparyāyā*|. This is also discussed by Jīva Gosvāmin in *Prīti-sandarbha* in paragraph 65.

[8] Śrī Rūpa Gosvāmin, *Bhakti-rasāmṛta-sindhu*, 1.3.1.

[9] ibid., 1.3.4.

edge, more than a particular methodology of study. But, methodology was also a consideration in the "science of religions." Since the word science in English has largely lost that older meaning, those who introduced the "scientific" study of religion into the academic scene in the United States preferred to call it the History of Religions. Thus, there seems no question at all but that *bhakti* should form a part of the study of the History of Religions. One might even designate a sub-area of that discipline that is devoted to the study of *bhakti* and call it *Bhaktiwissenschaft*. This book by Dr. Kapoor would certainly be an important contribution to that field. Using a kind of informal phenomenology as his methodology, Kapoor isolates four important features of *bhakti* as it has been experienced and written about in India. Continuing the metaphor of science, he refers to them as the Law of Gravitation, the Law of Reciprocation, the Law of Subjugation, and the Law of Unification. Using these terms, Kapoor attempts to unpack the relational dynamics that exist between the two parties involved in *bhakti*, the devotee, called the *bhakta*, and the Lord, called Bhagavān. One could apply the dynamics of *bhakti* and its principles to aspects of many religious traditions in other parts of the world. But this is not quite what Dr. Kapoor had in mind when he argues that *bhakti* is science.

Dr. Kapoor wants to argue that *bhakti* is "real" science, suggesting that what currently goes by the name of science is not real science. In arguing this, he has fallen into one of the old informal fallacies of logic: the fallacy of equivocation. The fallacy of equivocation is explained thus by Irving M. Copi:

> Most words have more than one literal meaning, as the word "pen" may denote either an instrument for writing or an enclosure for animals. When we keep these different meanings apart, no difficulty arises. But when we confuse the different meanings a single word or phrase may have, using it in different senses in the same context, we are using it equivocally. If the context happens to be an argument, we commit the Fallacy of Equivocation.[10]

Dr. Kapoor uses the word science in two different senses in the same context, the context of arguing that *bhakti* is science. One sense is the

[10] Irving M. Copi, *Introduction to Logic*, p. 113. (New York: Macmillan Publishing Company, 7th edition, 1986)

older sense of science mentioned above: a realm or body of knowledge on a particular subject. The other sense is that of science as it is used today for empirically verifiable, experimentally tested knowledge. One can agree with Dr. Kapoor that *bhakti* is science in the old sense but still disagree with him about *bhakti* being science in the modern sense. Why the equivocation? It is really science in the modern sense that has the prestige he wants *bhakti* to have,[11] not science in the old sense which was a mixture of knowledge, opinion, and belief. Thus, he says:

> But *bhakti* is science in a higher sense for the very reason that is it based on faith. It is a science just because, fundamentally and primarily, it is not the result of any experiments conducted by men, but because it is based on revelation or truths revealed to us by God himself, which are even more sure and certain than the conclusions of science, based on observation and experiments made by man with his limited understanding and senses.[12]

However, if *bhakti* is not the result of any experiments conducted by human beings, then it is not modern science, because knowledge experimentally verified on the basis of tests that are repeatable is what we mean by science today. Understanding based on revelation is not science; it is the result of faith. Some people think that faith means accepting something as true on the basis of no evidence whatsoever. It is doubtful, however, whether anyone's faith fits that extreme definition. There is always evidence of some sort. Maybe it is the evidence provided by the claims of respected friends or guides; maybe it is the evidence provided by the claims of a particular text that it is, say, the work or words of divinely inspired sages or indeed of some deity itself. There is always evidence of some sort. It may not be very good evidence, but there is always evidence. No one believes in anything without any evidence whatsoever. The strength of science is that it has raised the bar on what counts as good evidence and the results have been undeniably impressive, nothing short of spectacular.

One does need faith to accept a text as a revelation from some god. One needs faith to accept even the idea that there is a god in the first place, because, the evidence, though perhaps clear as day to some, is

[11] Kapoor, *Experiences in Bhakti*, Chapter 2, p. 9.
[12] ibid., p. 10.

nowhere to be found for others. Moreover, there is no way of verifying that a particular text is indeed a revelation from a god, and there is usually plenty of evidence suggesting that a text may not have any divine origin at all. Thus, there is no escaping the importance of faith in discussing religious ideas. As the great Latin theologian of early Christianity, Tertullian, said: "I believe because it is absurd; ... the fact is certain because it is impossible."[13]

Faith, called in Sanskrit *śraddhā*, is considered fundamentally important by the classic writers on *bhakti*. Śrī Rūpa Gosvāmin says, for instance, *ādau śraddhā*, "at the beginning there is [must be] faith."[14] Śrī Jīva, commenting on that passage, says: "In the beginning, that is, at first, through hearing the scriptures and associating with holy persons, there arises faith, which amounts to confidence in the meaning of those texts."[15] Śrī Mukunda Dāsa Gosvāmin commenting on the same passage says: "In the beginning, that is, first of all, by the arising of some kind of good fortune, there is faith in *bhakti* for Kṛṣṇa."[16] Mukunda Gosvāmin's comment highlights the mysterious and unpredictable nature of the arousal of faith: "by the arising of some kind of good fortune ... ." The authors of the *Bhāgavata* express a similar point of view with the word *yadṛcchayā*, "by chance ... ."[17]

All of these writers, however, assure their readers that in spite of the faith's roots being shrouded in mystery, those who follow the path or process can expect eventual verification of its truth. As a result of the next two steps after faith, association with the holy or good and engagement in the practices (which are learned from the holy) of worship or meditation, one eventually reaches the stages of cessation of harm-

---

[13]Tertullian, *On the Flesh of Christ*, Chapter Five. A more accurate representation of his words is: "The Son of God was crucified; I am not ashamed because men must needs be ashamed of it. And the Son of God died; it is by all means to be believed, because it is absurd. And He was buried, and rose again; the fact is certain, because it is impossible." Translation by Dr. Holmes. Kirby, Peter. "Tertullian." Early Christian Writings. 2006. 16 Nov. 2006 *http://www.earlychristianwritings.com/tertullian.html*.

[14]Śrī Rūpa, *Bhakti-rasāmṛta-sindhu*, 1.4.15.

[15]Śrī Jīva Gosvāmin, *Durgamasaṅgamanī*, on 1.4.15: *ādau prathame sādhusaṅga-śāstraśravaṇadvārā śraddhā tadarthaviśvāsaḥ*.

[16]Śrī Mukunda Dāsa Gosvāmin, *Artha-ratnālpa-dīpikā*, on 1.4.15: *ādau prthamaṃ kenāpi bhāgyodayena śrīkṛṣṇasya bhaktau śraddhā*.

[17]Bhāg. 11.20.8: *yadṛcchayā matkathādau jātaśraddhastu yaḥ pumān| na nirviṇṇo nātisakto bhaktiyogo'sya siddhidaḥ||*, "For a person who by chance has developed faith in stories about me [Kṛṣṇa] and such, without being too despondent or too attached, his discipline of *bhakti* brings him success."

ful habits and inclinations, characterized by Mukunda Gosvāmin as the results of past sinful acts that either already have begun to manifest or that have not yet begun to appear. After that, a firmness or steadiness, *niṣṭhā*, arises which Śrī Jīva describes as "constancy [in practice] without interruption," (*tatrāvikṣepeṇa sātatyam*). As these results begin to appear the process which was initially undertaken on very slim evidence becomes increasingly verified through the personal experiences of the practitioner. This is especially true when the preferences or tastes (*ruci*) of the practitioner begin to shift gradually in the next stage away from other interests towards Kṛṣṇa and when one becomes spontaneously drawn or attached to all things relating to Kṛṣṇa in the stage after that.

The system of the unfolding of *bhakti* or, as it is known in its fullest manifestation, of *preman* (selfless love), as described by Śrī Rūpa was almost certainly the result of his own lived experiences and of his own observation of the experiences of those around him. Thus, while one may hesitate to call *bhakti* science, one must insist that like science it results in verification in the experience of the practitioner. The goal is direct, unmediated experience, *aparokṣa-anubhūti*. Unlike science, however, which is practiced in the public sphere and is very much a part of our shared public life, *bhakti* is a private, inner affair. It is very difficult, if not impossible, to present such experiences and to measure their quality and intensity in the public domain. Hook a *bhakta* up to EEGs or MRIs and one will certainly find the neurons firing in certain recognizable patterns, but how those patterns are experienced from the inside by the person undergoing them is impossible to know. That is why Śrī Rūpa concludes that *bhakti* is very difficult to comprehend even for the brightest and most learned:

> Fortunate is the one in whose mind this new love (*preman*) unfolds! It's seal is extremely hard to crack even by those who know the inner meanings.[18]

And Śrī Jīva has this comment:

> Here is the idea: those learned in scripture have determined that the objects of human life are finding happiness and

---

[18] Rūpa Gosvāmin, ibid., 1.4.17:

> *dhanyasyāyaṃ navaḥ premā yasyonmīlati cetasi|*
> *antarvāṇibhbhirapyasya mudrā suṣṭthu sudurgamā||*

> avoiding distress. And they recognize those for *bhaktas*, too, only on the external level, not internally. Internally the *bhakta's* happiness and distress are caused by finding Bhagavān or not finding Bhagavān.[19]

He then cites two verses in support of his comment from the *Bhāgavata*:

> They do not consider final release to be your blessing, nor attaining any other high abode wherein fear is created by the mere raising of your eyebrows, those who, dear one, have surrendered at your feet and who are skillful tasters of the delight (*rasa*) of stories about you which are worthy of repeating and which are famous as purifying.
>
> We much prefer existence in the hells because of our sins, if our minds may delight in your lotus feet like bees [do in flowers], and if our words are beautified by your feet like leaves of *tulasī*, and the holes of our ears are filled with crowds of your merits.[20]

For some, too, there may be another problem with calling *bhakti* a science. Science refers to a body of knowledge and traditionally knowledge, called in Sanskrit *jñāna*, has been contrasted with or opposed by *bhakti*. There are thought, for instance, to be three distinct paths to the highest goal: the path of action (*karman*), the path of knowledge (*jñāna*) and the path of devotion (*bhakti*). How is it then that Dr. Kapoor tries to identify *bhakti* with science or a kind of knowledge.

In describing *bhakti* as a kind of knowledge, Dr. Kapoor is actually in very good company. The idea that *bhakti* is a kind of knowledge goes

---

[19]On Brs., 1.4.18: *ayaṃ bhāvaḥ śāstravidbhirhi sukha-prāpti-duḥkha-hānī eva puruṣārthatvena nirṇīte| te ca tādṛśabhaktānāṃ bahireva tairjñāyete, nāntaḥ, teṣāmantastu sukhaduḥkhe bhagavatprāptyaprāptikṛte eva|*

[20]Bhāg., 3.15.48-49:

> *nātyantikaṃ vigaṇayantyapi te prasādaṃ*
> *kimvānyadarpitabhayaṃ bhruva unnayaiste|*
> *ye'ṅga tvadaṅghriśaraṇā bhavataḥ kathāyāḥ*
> *kīrtanyatīrthayaśasaḥ kuśalā rasajñāḥ||*
>
> *kāmaṃ bhavaḥ svavṛjinairnirayeṣu naḥ stā-*
> *cceto'livadyadi nu te padayo rameta|*
> *vācaśca nastulasivadyadi te'ṅghriśobhāḥ*
> *pūryeta te guṇagaṇairyadi karṇarandhraḥ||*

way back in the history of the development of the idea. The earliest writer we know of who regarded *bhakti* as a kind of knowledge was Śaṅkara (650-700 CE) who is his commentary on *Bhagavad-gītā* 12.20 characterized the highest form of *bhakti* as "knowledge of the highest truth" (*uttamāṃ paramārthajñānalakṣaṇāṃ bhaktim*).[21] This kind of *bhakti* is paired in the *Gītā* with the adjective *uttamā* which means the "highest" or "most elevated." So the highest form of *bhakti* Śaṅkara regarded as a kind of knowledge, not just any kind of knowledge but the very kind that was for him the most significant kind, knowledge of the highest truth. That is the kind of knowledge that destroys the ignorance that keeps living beings bound to the cycle of birth and death. it is, therefore, liberating knowledge.

The next major thinker who recognized *bhakti* as a kind of knowledge was Rāmānuja, the foremost teacher of the South Indian Vaiṣṇava community called the Śrī Sampradāya. He discusses *bhakti* in his book *Vedārtha-saṅgraha* (Collection of the Teachings of the Vedas). There he cites a famous passage from the *Īśāvāsya Upaniṣad* (11):

> One who knows both knowledge and ignorance together crosses over death by means of ignorance and gains immortality by means of knowledge.[22]

He takes ignorance or non-knowledge (*a-vidyā*) as that which is other than knowledge, or, in other words, as action in the form of the practices of the caste and stage-of-life system (*varṇāśrama*) of Hindu social organization. Knowledge, however, means meditation which has reached the form of *bhakti.* Pointing to a number of Upaniṣadic passages, he says that knowing or *vedana* means meditating. To further support his case he cites another famous Upaniṣadic passage from the *Kaṭha Upaniṣad* (1.2.22) and the *Muṇḍaka Upaniṣad* (3.2.3):

> This Self is not attainable by means of speech, nor by sharp intellect, nor by having heard much. It is attained by someone whom this one [the Self] chooses. To such a one this Self reveals its [the Self's] own body.[23]

[21]Śaṅkara, *Bhagavad-gītā-bhāṣya*, 12.20.

[22]*Īśāvāsya Upaniṣad.* 11:

> *vidyāṃ cāvidyāṃ ca yattadvedobhayaṃ saha|*
> *avidyayā mṛtyuṃ tīrtvā vidyayāmṛtamaśnute||*

[23]*Kaṭha Upaniṣad*, 1.2.22 and *Muṇḍaka Upaniṣad*, 3.2.3:

Rāmānuja takes this verse to mean that the Self is attained by means of meditation which has reached the state of *bhakti*, not by mere knowing. This is so because mere knowing is excluded by the words *na medhayā*, "not by sharp intellect." The verse claims, according to Rāmānuja, that someone desiring liberation should practice meditation, a form of knowing, as prescribed by the Vedānta texts. When an affection or a liking (*prīti*) for that meditation is born then he attains the Supreme Person. To add support to his interpretation Rāmānuja quotes the words of Bhagavān Kṛṣṇa himself from the *Gītā* (8.22, 11.54, and 18.55):

> This highest spirit, Pṛthā's son,
> In whom all creatures do abide,
> By whom pervaded is the world,
> Is reached by undivided love.
>
> But I may yet be known like this,
> By love on me alone bestowed,
> And known and seen, too, as I am,
> And entered into, Parantap.
>
> By such devotion such a one
> Knows who and what I am in truth,
> And knowing me in truth, he then
> Finds entrance into me forthwith.[24]

The word being translated in these verse by "undivided love," "love," and "devotion" is *bhakti*. Rāmānuja summarizes his understanding of

---

> *nāyaṃ pravacanena labhyaḥ na medhayā na bahunā śrutena|*
> *yamevaiṣa vṛṇute tena labhyaḥ tasyaiṣa ātmā vivṛṇute tanūṃ svām|*

Interestingly, Śaṅkara switches the subject for the second line making it the practitioner who chooses the Self and the Self who reveals its own body or true nature to the practitioner in response. Most everyone else understands the Self to be the one doing the choosing.

[24]*Bhagavad-gītā*:

> *puruṣaḥ sa paraḥ pārtha bhaktyā labhyastvananyayā|*
> *yasyāntaḥsthāni bhūtāni yena sarvam idaṃ tatam|| 8.22||*
>
> *bhaktyā tvananyayā śakya aham evaṃvidho 'rjuna|*
> *jñātuṃ draṣṭuṃ ca tattvena praveṣṭuṃ ca paraṃtapa|| 11.54||*
>
> *bhaktyā māṃ abhijānāti yāvān yaścāsmi tattvataḥ|*
> *tato māṃ tattvato jñātvā viśate tadanantaram|| 18.55||*

Translation by C. C. Caleb in *The Song Divine or, Bhagavad-gītā: a metrical rendering.* (Kirksville, MO: Blazing Sapphire Press, 2011) "Parantap" is a name of Arjuna meaning "scorcher of the enemy."

bhakti by saying that it is a special kind of knowledge that is extremely dear, has no other purpose besides itself, and produces a lack of desire for everything else.[25] Someone who possesses such *bhakti* becomes worthy of being chosen by the Supreme Self and thus the Supreme Self "chooses" one, as the verse says.

Rāmānuja sums up his position later in the text when he says:

> And the way to attainment of Brahman is the highest *bhakti* in the form of meditation which has reached the state of direct perception (*pratyakṣatā*) of the clearest sort and which is extremely delightful. Such *bhakti* is the goal of the unflagging practice of *bhakti* which is aided by the performance of one's appointed actions, preceded by knowledge of the truths learned from scripture. The word *bhakti* means a special kind of love (*prīti*) and that love is a special kind of knowledge.[26]

Here we see that *bhakti* or rather the highest *bhakti* is believed to culminate in a kind of extremely clear direct perception growing out of meditation, thus making it without doubt a kind of knowledge.

For the views of another, later poet-thinker who characterizes *bhakti* in a similar way, we turn again to Śrī Rūpa Gosvāmin (1470-1554 CE) of the Caitanya tradition. He says, in his *Ocean of the Nectar of Sacred Rapture* (*Bhakti-rasāmṛta-sindhu*):

> A special kind of pure being (*śuddha-sattva*), similar to a beam from the sun of divine love (*preman*), which softens the mind with its rays, is called feeling (*bhāva*, or as we also call it, attraction, *rati*). It appears in an operation of the mind (*manovṛtti*) and becomes one with it. Though it is a form of illumination (light) it appears like something to be illumined, and though that attraction (*rati*) is in reality of the very nature of enjoyment itself it becomes the cause of the enjoyment of Kṛṣṇa and the rest.[27]

---

[25] *bhaktirapi niratiśaya-priyānanyaprayojana-svetaravaitṛṣṇyāvaha-jñānaviśeṣa eva*

[26] *Vedārtha-saṅgraha* (Vas), para 238: *brahmaprāptyupāyaśca śāstrādhigata-tattvajñānapūrvaka-svakarmānugṛhīta-bhaktiniṣṭhā-sādhyānavadhikātiśaya-priyaviśadatama-pratyakṣatāpannānudhyāna-rūpa-paramabhaktir eva ityuktam| bhaktiśabdaśca prītiveśeṣe vartate| prītiśca jñānaviśeṣa eva|*

[27] Brs., 1.3.1 and 1.3.4-5:

Bhakti's being a form of knowledge is clear from its connection with the mental operations or functions, *manovṛtti*. *Manovṛttis* are the contents, ideas or faculties of the mind and are the sources of all our knowledge. Here *bhakti* appears among the mental operations from somewhere outside them and though it is different from them it becomes one with them in nature. Though *bhakti* is illumination itself it appears like the other mental operations as objects of illumination. Though it is enjoyment or tasting itself it appears as the cause of the enjoyment or tasting whose object is Kṛṣṇa and the rest (his companions, sports, and so forth). The upshot of what Rūpa is saying here it that *bhakti* is a kind of consciousness (*cit*), because consciousness is the illuminator of other unconscious objects and *bhakti* is a kind of very enjoyable experience which is coded by the word *āsvāda* or "tasting." Nevertheless, it appears like an object of consciousness in need of illumination by consciousness or like an object of experience.

Commenting on these verses, Rūpa's nephew, Jīva Gosvāmin (1508-1592? CE), who was the main systematic theologian of the Caitanya tradition, says:

> "That *rati* (attraction), which is a special kind of pure being and is called *rati* because *rati* is its main operation or function (*vṛtti*), is itself a form of illumination because it illuminates or reveals everything relating to Kṛṣṇa and the rest (i.e., his companions, sports, names, etc). Though it is illumination itself, it nevertheless appears as a mental operation of Kṛṣṇa's dear *bhaktas* in the phenomenal world, becomes identical with it (the mental operation) and seems to be illumined by that operation like Brahman's appearing in a mental operation [and appearing to be illumined by it]. Moreover, by being united [with that mental operation] it takes the form of cause and effect through its prior and later states, that *rati*, which is also called *bhāva* or strong feeling, becomes the most effective means, through its conscious-

---

śuddhasattvaviśeṣātmā premasūryāṃśusāmyabhāk|
rucibhiścittamāsṛṇyakṛdasau bhāva ucyate||
āvirbhūya manovṛttau vrajantī tatsvarūpatām|
svayamprakāśarūpāpi bhāsamānā prakāśyavat||
vastutaḥ svayamāsvādasvarūpaiva ratistvasau|
kṛṣṇādikarmakāsvādahetutvaṃ pratipadyate||

ness part (*saṃvid-aṃśa*), of bringing about the perception of the sweetness of Bhagavān (Kṛṣṇa) and the rest, and thus becomes the cause of the tasting or enjoyment of those objects, Kṛṣṇa and the rest which are forms of taste itself and which are most desirable to the agent of that tasting [i.e., the *bhakta*]. Moreover, through its pleasure-giving part it causes pleasure as well."[28]

This is a difficult passage because so much is packed into it. Nevertheless, Śrī Jīva clearly understands *bhakti* as having two parts or aspects which he identifies as *saṃvit* and *hlādinī*. *Saṃvit* is the consciousness- or awareness-creating and *hlādinī* is the pleasure-giving power. These correspond to the illuminating or revealing and the enjoying or tasting functions of *bhakti* in Śrī Rūpa's original verses. Thus, *bhakti* is a kind of knowledge that reveals Kṛṣṇa and causes him to be tasted or enjoyed. Interestingly, Śrī Jīva compares the appearance of *bhakti* in the mental operation of the *bhakta* with the appearance of Brahman in the mental operation of the knower pursuing liberation. Brahman enters the mental operation, becomes one with it, that is to say, the mental operation takes the form of Brahman, which means that Brahman becomes the object of that mental operation. That last mental operation is called *akhaṇḍākārākāritā*, the mental operation shaped by unfragmented form. It is the direct knowledge of Brahman which destroys the root ignorance of the living being. Part of that root ignorance is that last mental operation itself and as a result it, too, is destroyed leading to the release of the living being.[29] It is interesting to see how *bhakti* has absorbed into itself or replaced the knowing and liberating capacity of *jñāna* (liberating knowledge) so important to the older Advaita Vedānta tradition. Nowhere is this more clear in than in the work of the late Advaita Vedāntin, Madhusūdana Sarasvatī (1540-1630 CE).

Madhusūdana Sarasvatī comes near the end of a long development in the Advaita Vedānta tradition in which *bhakti* gradually becomes

[28]Śrī Jīva, comm. on 1.3.4-5: *asau śuddhasattvaviśeṣarūpā ratirmūlarūpatvena mukhyavṛttyā tacchabdavācyā sā ratiḥ śrīkṛṣṇādisarvaprakāśakatvena hetunā svaymprakāśarūpāpi prāpañcikatatpriyajanānāṃ manovṛttau āvirbhūya tatsvarūpatāṃ tattādātmyaṃ vrajantī tadvṛttyā prakāśyavadbhāsamānā brahmavattasyāṃ sphuratī tathā svasātkṛtena pūrvottarāvasthābhyāṃ kāraṇakāryarūpeṇa śrībhagavadādimādhuryānubhavena svāṃśenāsvādarūpāṇi yāni Kṛṣṇādirūpāṇi karmāṇi karturīpsitatamāni teṣāmāsvādahetutāṃ saṃvidaṃśena sādhakatamatāmasau bhāvaikaparyayā ratiḥ pratipadyate prāpnotīti*|

[29]This is discussed in more detail in the *Vedānta-sāra* of Sadānanda Yogīndra, paragraph 124. See my translation of the passage in *The Fundamentals of Vedānta*, 129-130.

a highly respected and respectable feature of practice and ideology. Though recognized in Śaṅkara as valuable, as we have seen, *bhakti* did not play a particularly large or important role in his his philosophy. Śaṅkara primarily discusses *bhakti* in his commentary on the *Bhagavad-gītā* where *bhakti* is a frequent and central topic. His discussion of it in that context is almost forced upon him by the nature of the text he is commenting on. Apart from that, however, *bhakti* is scarcely mentioned in Śaṅkara's other authentic works. Nevertheless, over the course of centuries *bhakti* assumes a more central place in the thinking of Advaitin philosophers, until one finds it emerge in writers like Vopadeva (13th cent.), Śrīdhara Svāmī and Lakṣmīdhara Svāmī (both 14th cent. CE) as a major object of discussion and feature of the path to liberation. These writers were no doubt influenced by the Advaitic theism of the *Viṣṇu* and *Bhāgavata Purāṇas* and perhaps, too, by the rich poetic developments in Kṛṣṇaism evident in works like Jayadeva's *Gīta-govindam* (13th century CE) and Bilvamaṅgala's *Kṛṣṇa-karṇāmṛta* (14th century CE).[30] One might argue that this development reached a kind of peak in works and philosophies of Advaitin renunciants like Viṣṇu and Mādhavendra Purī.[31] Madhusūdana Sarasvatī, being a Bengali, is also likely to have benefited in his understanding of *bhakti* from the powerful movement of ecstatic *bhakti* of Śrī Kṛṣṇacaitanya (an Advaitin *brahmacārin*, or renunciant in training, of the Bhāratī order) which blossomed in Bengal during his lifetime. There is no clear evidence that Madhusūdana studied any of the works on *bhakti-rasa* written by Śrī Caitanya's followers, Śrī Rūpa and Śrī Jīva, but his views as we shall see are very similar to theirs in many respects and those works were probably available to him during his active years.

If we look at the opening verse in Madhusūdana's *Elixir of Bhakti* (*Bhakti-rasāyana*) we find striking similarities between his view and that

[30]The roots of this poetic development featuring love poetry focused on the erotic love of Rādhā and Kṛṣṇa can be traced back to Hāla's Prakrit work, the *Gāthā-saptaśatī* (2nd cent. CE?), in which Rādhikā, Kṛṣṇa's lover, appears for the first time by name.

[31]Some believe that these two members of Śaṅkarite Daśanāmī orders (ten interrelated orders of renunciants, supposedly founded by Śaṅkara, with ten lineage names, among which are found both Purī and Sarasvatī) at some point converted to the Madhva tradition. As far as I can tell, there is absolutely no evidence for this claim. The fact that these writers held *bhakti* in high esteem is far more likely a result of developments within the Advaita tradition itself, than a result of the influence of Madhva or any of the other Vaiṣṇava traditions. For one thing, the views of these writers on *bhakti* show no particular allegiance or similarity to those of Madhva or his tradition.

of the Caitanya tradition. The first verse reads:

> Either with the nine *rasas*, or,
> By itself, *bhakti-yoga* for
> Mukunda they here proclaim
> As humanity's highest aim.
> It, through scripture's view, I reveal
> For everybody's joy and weal,
> As it is untouched by misery,
> Formed of unmatched bliss and consciousness.[32]

Several ideas are suggested here. First of all the idea that *bhakti* is the highest goal or aim of humanity is very reminiscent of the main teachings attributed to Śrī Caitanya by his close disciples. The famous verse by Śrīnātha Cakravartin gives it as a central and perhaps distinctive doctrine:

> To be worshiped is Bhagavān,
> the son of the Lord of Vraja,
> and his region Vṛndāvana.
> Delightful is the form of service
> devised by the wives of Vraja.
> Scripture means the *Bhāgavata*,
> a flawless method of knowing;
> divine love is the great goal of humankind.
> Such is the view
> of Gaura Mahāprabhu.
> Therefore, to it goes our highest respect.[33] (1)

---

[32]Madhusūdana Sarasvatī, *Bhakti-rasāyana*, 1.1:

> *navarasamilitaṃ vā kevalaṃ vā pumartham*
> *paramamiha mukunde bhaktiyogaṃ vadanti|*
> *nirupamasukhasaṃvidrūpamaspṛṣṭaduḥkham*
> *tamahamakhilatuṣṭyai śāstradṛṣṭyā vyanajmi|*

[33]Śrīnātha Cakravartin, *Śrī Caitanya-mata-mañjuṣā*, 1.1.1:

> *ārādhyo bhagavān vrajeśatanayastaddhāma vṛndāvanaṃ*
> *ramyā kācidupāsanā vrajavadhūvargeṇa yā kalpitā|*
> *śāstraṃ bhāgavataṃ pramāṇamamalaṃ premā pumartho mahān*
> *itthaṃ gauramahāprabhormatamatastatrādaro naḥ paraḥ|| 1||*

Here divine love or *prema* is given as the highest goal of humanity, but *prema* is just another name for *bhakti*. This runs counter to the idea that there are only four goals for mankind: sensual pleasure, wealth, piety, and liberation. Śrī Caitanya is famous for introducing another goal, divine love, the fifth and highest goal. Madhusūdana is a little vague when he says "they here proclaim." Who proclaims and where? It probably was the Caitanyites among others whom Madhusūdana had in mind. In his auto-commentary on that first verses he glosses the "they" with "knowers of rasa," or *rasajña*. "Here" could meaning either in Vārāṇasī where Madhusūdana lived most of his life, or in Bengal, more specifically in Navadvīpa in Bengal, the birthplace of Śrī Caitanya, where Madhusūdana is said to have gotten his early education.

The fact that Madhusūdana refers to only nine *rasas* instead of Śrī Rūpa's twelve *rasas* (the primary five plus secondary seven *bhakti-rasas*) means either that he had not read Rūpa's work or that he had and nevertheless preferred to stick to the traditional view, the view he inherited from the Advaitin tradition through Vopadeva and Śrīdhara. Even early writers in the Caitanya tradition like Śrīnātha Cakravartin and his disciple Kavi Karṇapūra stuck to the nine rasa tradition.

More important for our discussion here of the history of the recognition of *bhakti* as a form of knowledge is what Madhusūdana says about *bhakti* in this verse. He says that *bhakti* has the form of "unmatched bliss and consciousness" (*nirupama-sukha-saṃvid-rūpa*). Bliss and consciousness are the same as the pleasure-giving (*hlādinī*) power and the consciousness-giving (*saṃvit*) power we found in the works of Śrī Rūpa and Śrī Jīva before. The identification of *bhakti* with consciousness or awareness makes it a form of knowledge. The connection of *bhakti* with knowledge is made even clearer when we look at Madhusūdana's definition of *bhakti* in the third verse of his book:

> Melted because of Bhagavān's
> *Dharma*, it streams without a break
> Towards the Controller of All.
> That mental spin is called *bhakti*.[34]

[34] ibid., 1.3:

> *drutasya bhagavaddharmāddhārāvāhikatāṃ gatā|*
> *sarveśe manaso vṛttirbhaktirityabhidhīyate||*

Like Rūpa, Madhusūdana identifies *bhakti* with a mental operation or spin (*manovṛtti*). Mental operations are commonly the way knowledge is considered to arise in classical Indian philosophical thinking. For Rūpa the genesis of the mental operation that is known as *bhakti* is the internal power of Bhagavān called the pleasure-giving or *hlādinī* power which descends into the mind of the *bhakta* and becomes one with it at some point in his or her spiritual development. For Madhusūdana, as we shall see, it is the power of the object perceived that causes the mind to melt and then harden in the form of the powerful object. He says, for instance, in his next verse:

> The mind's substance is like shellac.
> In its natural state it's hard.
> In union with warming objects
> It reaches a state of melting.[35]

As Madhusūdana says in his auto-commentary on this verse:

> The excitants (*uddīpana*), such as desire, anger, and so forth which are conveyed by hearing of the qualities of Bhagavān, cause the mind to melt and its turn or spin (*vṛtti*) becoming a steady, unbroken stream directed to the Lord of All, takes the shape of Bhagavān. This taking the shape of an object is what is always meant by the word "turn" or "spin" (*vṛtti*) in our philosophy. Therefore, that is known as *bhakti* by those who know scripture. And scripture is thus:
>
> > By mere hearing of my qualities,
> > The flow of the mind towards me,
> > Who am in the heart of everyone,
> > Becomes unbroken, like the flow
> > Of Ganges water to the sea.
> > Unqualified *bhakti-yoga*'s
> > Definition is this indeed.[36]

---

[35]ibid., 1.4:

> *cittadravyaṃ tu jatuvatsvabhāvātkaṭhinātmakam|*
> *tāpakairviṣayairyoge dravatvaṃ pratipadyate||*

[36]ibid,. comm. on 1.3: *bagavadguṇaśravaṇena vakṣyamānakāmakrodhādyuddīpana-dvārā dravāvasthāṃ prāptasya cittasya dhārāvāhikī vā sarveśaviṣayā vṛttiḥ bhagavadākāra-*

Thus, for Madhusūdana, *bhakti* is a form of knowledge whose object is Bhagavān. More specifically, *bhakti* is a certain shape the mental operation or turn assumes in contact with its divine object. Since knowledge in the Śaṅkarite tradition has from the very beginning been the only means to liberation, Madhusūdana's claim that *bhakti*, which is a kind of knowledge, is also a means to liberation need not be seen as a departure from the teachings of his tradition at all. The Advaita Vedānta tradition, at least in some of its lines, clearly evolved to incorporate *bhakti* as a form of knowledge that brings liberation. Moreover, for Madhusūdana, the pleasurable nature of *bhakti* comes to the surface when it is tasted or enjoyed as *bhakti-rasa.* Thus, the dual-nature of *bhakti*, as both pleasure and knowledge, which can be traced in the understanding of *bhakti* all the way back to Śaṅkara, is also maintained in Madhusūdana Sarasvatī's formulation.

One final writer needs to be considered on this topic. Baladeva Vidyābhūṣaṇa was an 18th century member of the Caitanya tradition and also a scholar and prolific writer. He wrote the tradition's principal commentary on the *Brahma-sūtra* called the *Govinda-bhāṣya.* In a separate work, the *Jewel of Doctrine* (*Siddhānta-ratna*) which is often referred to as the introduction to his *Govinda-bhāṣya*, Baladeva refers to *bhakti* as a special kind of knowledge. Here is what he says:

> *Bhakti*, too, is a kind of knowledge because it shares the generic property knowledge-ness (*jñānatva*). Such is the intention in the statements: "Knowing him alone one passes beyond death. There is no other way to go (*Śvetāśvatara Upaniṣad*, 3.8)" and "But only knowledge [is the cause of liberation] because scripture mentions that (*Brahma-sūtra*, 3.3.4)." Putting the genus first one indicates the oneness in the many. As Bharata has said: "Because of the unlimitedness of *rasas*, they are counted as one category." That is explained in more detail [in my *Sāhitya-kaumudī* (Moonlight of Literature)]. After accepting the class that has no notice-

---

tetyarthaḥ, tadākārataiva hi sarvatra vṛttiśabdārtho'smākaṃ darśane, ataḥ sā bhaktirityabhidhīyate śāstravidbhiḥ| tathā ca śāstram—

madguṇaśrutimātreṇa mayi sarvaguhāśaye|
manogatiravicchinnā yathā gaṅgāmbhaso'mbudhau||
lakṣaṇaṃ bhaktiyogasya nirguṇasya hyudāhṛtam| (bhāg. 3.29.11-12)

> able sequence, *rasas* and such are counted as one. Otherwise, one would be unable to count each one because there are too many types. The word *bhakti* is used for a type of knowledge just like the word Pāṇḍava is used for a type of Kaurava.[37]

Thus, Baladeva argues that *bhakti* is a species in the general class of types of knowledge, just as the Pāṇḍavas are a species or sub-class of the Kaurava clan. He gives us more detail in his next paragraph:

> Here is a teasing out of the point—knowledge is of two kinds and is known by the names science (*vidyā*) and sensation (*vedana*). The first, which is like staring at something without blinking, has the form of perceiving the meanings of the "that" (*tat*) and the "you" (*tvam*) categories.[38] But the second which is more like viewing something with a sidelong glance is diverse and takes the form of *bhakti*. By focusing on the pure "you" category, a living being, though also a part of the "that" category, lacks the good fortune of the grace of Bhagavān, like a wife rejected by her husband, and gets liberation of the nature of isolation (*kaivalya*). As it is said in revelation (Bṛ. Ā. U., 1.4.12): "If a person comes to know the self saying 'I am this,' then wishing for what and for the desire of what, would he heat up his body?"[39]

So, through the direct approach to gaining knowledge, argues Baladeva, one approaches the absolute somewhat aggressively and as a result one gets, as his tradition conceives it, a lesser result, liberation in the form of isolation (*kaivalya*), if, that is, one contemplates most deeply

[37] Baladeva Vidyābhūṣaṇa, *Siddhānta-ratna*, 1.32: *bhaktirapi jñānaviśeṣo bhavatīti jñānatvasāmānyāt tameveti vidyaiveti ca vyapadeśaḥ| jātiṃ puraskṛtya bahuṣvaikyaṃ vyapadiśyate| yadāha bharataḥ—rasādīnāmanantatvādbhed eko hi gaṇyata iti| vivṛtañcaitadasaṃlakṣyakramatvaṃ jātimādāya rasādireka eva gaṇyate| anyathā tadgaṇanamaśakyam, pratyekaṃ bhedabāhulāditi| jñānaviśeṣe bhaktiśabdaprayogaḥ kauravaviśeṣe pāṇḍavaśabdavadbodhyaḥ||*

[38] In the famous Upaniṣadic statement: "that you are" or "you are that" (*tat tvam asi*). It is considered one of the greatest teachings or *mahāvākyas* of the Upaniṣads.

[39] ibid., 1.33: *ayamatra niṣkarṣaḥ—vidyāvedanaparyyāyaṃ jñānaṃ dvividham| ekaṃ nirnimeṣavīkṣaṇavattattvampadārthānubhavarūpam| dvitīyaṃ tu apāṅgavīkṣaṇavadvicitraṃ bhaktirūpamiti| tatra śuddhatvampadārthānusandhināsya jīvasya tatpadabhājo'pi patityaktapatnīvadbhagavatprasādasaubhāgyahīnasya kaivalyalakṣaṇo mokṣaḥ syāt| (bṛ. ā. u., 4.4.12) ātmānaṃ cedvijānīyādayamasmīti puruṣaḥ| kimicchan kasya kāmāya śarīramanusaṃjvarediti śruteḥ|*

the "you" or *tvam* part of the Upaniṣadic great statement, *tat tvam asi*. The idea that this is a lesser result is communicated through the example of the rejected wife. A rejected wife has knowledge of her husband but not his grace or approval. Similarly, a knower of the "you" but not the "that" has some knowledge of the absolute but not its grace. If, instead, one focuses more deeply on the "that" or *tat* part of the statement then:

> From specially pure knowledge of the "that" category, however, one partakes of the good fortune of his grace, like a minister, or general or such does of that of the king, and gets liberation of the nature of location in the same abode as the Lord, and so forth.[40] This teaching comes from the statement of revelation[41] beginning from: "That, indeed, Satyakāma," upto "once again, if one would meditate on the supreme person by means of the syllable *oṃ* with its three measures (a, u, m), he would become perfectly accomplished in the fiery sun and be liberated like a snake from its skin. He, thus, being liberated from sin is raised by the Sāman hymns to the world of Brahmā. He sees the person who is beyond this collection of living beings in the highest heaven." Here and elsewhere, however, scriptural knowledge should be accepted as the doorway. Otherwise, the inclination to try for this would not arise.[42]

Thus, according to Baladeva, knowledge of the "you" leads to the liberation of solitude and knowledge of the "that" leads to one of the four types of liberation. So far we have been addressing the type of knowledge called *vidyā* or, as I have translated it, "science." This is not, of course, the science of the present day, but science as a careful direct

---

[40] These are the four forms of liberation: achieving the same world (*sālokya*), achieving the same form (*sārūpya*), achieving the presence of the Lord (*sāmīpya*) and becoming one with the Lord (*sāyujya*).

[41] *Praśna Upaniṣad*, 5.2-5

[42] ibid., 1.34: *tatpadārthapariśuddhavijñānāttu amātyasainyādhipādivad yathāyathaṃ tatprasādasaubhāgyabhājanasya tasya sālokyādilakṣaṇā muktirbhavati| etadvai satyakāma paraṃ cāparaṃ brahma yadoṅkāraḥ ityupakramya, yaḥ punaretaṃ trimātreṇaivaumityetenaivākṣareṇa paraṃ puruṣamabhidhyāyīta| sa tejasi sūrye sampanno yathā pādodarastvacā vinirmucyate| evaṃ ha vai sa pāpmanā vinirmuktaḥ sa sāmabhirunnīyate brahmalokaṃ| sa etasmājjīvaghanāt parāt paraṃ puriśayaṃ puruṣamīkṣate iti śravaṇāt| śāstrīyaṃ jñānaṃ tu atra paratra ca dvārabhūtaṃ svīkāryaṃ| itarathā pravṛttyanupapatteḥ||*

study of any subject. In this case, since we are in the realm of Vedānta, the object of study is a teaching from one of the Upaniṣads, perhaps the most important of the great teachings (*mahāvākya*), "you are that" (*tat tvam asi*). The other kind of knowing is called *vedana* which is hard to translate. It means sensing, or feeling, or becoming aware of something indirectly, or perhaps even intuiting something. Thus, the example of observing something or someone through sidelong glances is given. This is the kind of knowing or knowledge *bhakti* is. It appears to be a more intimate form of knowledge:

> By means of the kind of knowledge having the form of *bhakti*, however, a person who is the recipient of the grace that subdues Bhagavān—like a jewel of a woman endowed with affection, beauty and other good qualities—gains the object of human life in the form of the joy of serving him directly.[43] "*Bhakti* alone leads to this one. *Bhakti* reveals this one. The supreme person is controlled by *bhakti*. *Bhakti* alone is greater."[44] "[Kṛṣṇa's form of] condensed consciousness and bliss stands in *bhakti yoga*, which is the same as being, consciousness and bliss."[45] And from tradition, we have:[46] "I am subservient to my *bhaktas* as if I were not independent, o twice-born. My heart is held by the holy *bhaktas* and I am dear to my *bhaktas*. The holy ones' hearts are bound to me, those who see all beings as equal. They bring me under their control by their *bhakti* like a good wife does her good husband."[47]

---

[43]The actual phrase is "serving his feet" (*tad-aṅghri-varivasyā*) It means direct service. The expression leaves lots of room for misunderstanding when rendered literally into English.

[44]Baladeva says this is from the "*Tāpanī-śruti*" in his auto-commentary on this passage. I have not been able to find it in the printed version of the *Gopāla-tāpanī* that I have. Since he did not specifically say "*Gopāla-tāpanī*" as he did for the next citation, it may be in the other *tāpanī*, the *Rāma-tāpanī Upaniṣad*. I have not been able to test this theory. I have found some references that suggest that it was cited by Madhvācārya in his commentary on *Brahma-sūtra*, at 3.3.53. but I have not been able to consult that text.

[45]*Gopāla-tāpanī* Uttara, 79.

[46]*Bhāg.* 9.4.63,66.

[47]ibid., 1.35: *bhaktirūpeṇa tu jñānaviśeṣeṇa snehasaundaryādiguṇāñcitayuvatīratnavadbhagavadvaśīkāraprasādapātrasya tadaṅghrivarivasyānandalakṣaṇaḥ puruṣārtho bhavati| bhaktirevainaṃ nayati, bhaktirevainaṃ darśayati, bhaktivaśaḥ puruṣo bhaktireva bhūyasīti, vijñānaghanānandaghanā saccidānandaikarase bhaktiyoge tiṣṭhatīti ca gopālatāpanīyaśrutāḥ|*

Having thus established that *bhakti* is a kind of knowledge, a subtler, more intimate way of knowing better described as "sensing" than as direct, measured observation, and that it is able to make the Lord submissive to whomever has it, Baladeva now points out its desirelessness (*niṣkāmatva*), in the sense that nothing other than *bhakti* is desired:

> The desire for the forms of liberation mentioned before does not arise from *bhakti* itself as is stated in the tradition:[48] "Though the four kinds of liberation headed by inhabiting the same world are known by service to me, they [the *bhaktas*] do not want them, being fulfilled by that service, to say nothing of any other thing that will be lost in time." And even in the definition of *bhakti* this is found in the *Atharvaśiras Upaniṣad*:[49] "*Bhakti* is the worship (*bhajana*) of him [Kṛṣṇa] and that is without adjuncts (*upādhi*) in this world or in the next. It is the fixing of the mind in him without attachment to results." And from the *Nārada-pañcarātra*: "Serving Hṛṣīkeśa ["Lord of the Senses," Kṛṣṇa] with the senses in a manner that is free of all adjuncts and that is pure because only intent on that is called the highest form of *bhakti*."[50]

Baladeva continues his discussion of *bhakti*, the details of which need not detain us here. His conclusion, however, is the following:

> And thus it is demonstrated that the essential core of the united pleasure-giving and consciousness powers is *bhakti*. And its being the essential core means that it is a special desire favorable to the ones in Kṛṣṇa's eternal companions. It is with such *bhakti* in mind that revelation distinguishes it as the same as being, consciousness, and bliss.[51] And it

---

ahaṃ bhaktaparādhīno hyasvatantra iva dvija| sādhubhirgrastahṛdayo bhaktairbhaktajanapriyaḥ|| mayi nirbaddhahṛdayāḥ sādhavaḥ samadarśinaḥ| vaśe karuvanti māṃ bhaktyā satstriyaḥ satpatiṃ yathetyādismṛteśca||

[48] Bhāg., 9.4.67.

[49] *Gopāla-tāpanī Upaniṣad*, Pūrva, 15.

[50] ibid., 36: *sālokyādestu nehābhilāṣaḥ svataḥ sambhavāt (bhāg. 9.4.67) matsevayā pratītaṃ te sālokyādicatuṣṭayam| necchanti sevayā pūrṇāḥ kuto'nyatkālaviplutamiti smṛteḥ| bhaktilakṣaṇe'pyevaṃ pathyate (goḥ tāḥ) bhaktirasya bhajanaṃ tadihāmutropādhinairāsyeṇāmusmin manaḥkalpanameva naiṣkarmyamityatharvaśarasi| sarvopādhivinirmuktaṃ tatparatvena nirmalaṃ| hṛṣīkeṇa hṛṣīkeśasevanaṃ bhaktiruttamā iti nāradapañcarātre ca||*

[51] In the passage from the *Gopāla-tāpanī Upaniṣad* cited before.

> shows the Lord's being controlled there, too, in the passage beginning with "condensed consciousness ... ," and in the passage "*bhakti*, alone, leads to him."[52]

Building on a long tradition of teaching on *bhakti* stretching back over a thousand years, Baladeva concludes that it is a form of knowledge distinct from other forms of knowledge and that it is at the same time an intensely pleasurable form. Thus, as implausible as Dr. Kapoor's thesis, that *bhakti* is a kind of science, may have seemed at the outset, given the universe of discourse within which he situated himself and operated, it makes sense and is justifiable for him to think and talk of *bhakti* as a science. The body of knowledge made accessible through the special form of knowledge called *bhakti* can be called a science. To be sure, others who do not have high regard for this tradition of discourse will deny that *bhakti* is any kind of knowledge at all. No one can really blame them for this. Nevertheless, even they have to agree that given the assumptions accepted by Dr. Kapoor, his reasoning is sound.

Bhakti, then, is regarded by those traditions that paid attention to it as a special kind of knowledge. Though this is so, it is, as are other forms of knowledge, difficult to verify. I said previously that it was a kind of state of mind, a type of pleasurable awareness that comes from believing oneself to be in relationship with Bhagavān. As a state of mind, its results in speech, action, and physical reaction are sometimes indistinguishable from the results of other states of mind. And there is no way to be certain what is in someone's heart. It may contain *bhakti* or it may contain some other motivating factor. There is as far as we currently know no neuron complex unique to *bhakti* that can be identified and measured and that proves someone is in a state of *bhakti*, a state of intense feeling related with the supreme being. If one cannot tell with any certainty if someone has *bhakti*, one cannot tell if what that person does or says is an example or result of *bhakti*. If one cannot tell if something is a result of *bhakti*, one does not know if it is supportive of the laws of *bhakti*. Therefore, the evidence that Dr. Kapoor musters may not really be proof of anything much. It is anecdotal, not the result of carefully controlled, experimental observations and gathering of data.

---

[52]ibid., 40: *tathā ca hlādasaṃvidoḥ samavetayoḥ sāro bhaktiriti sidhyati| tatsāratvaṃ ca tannityaparikarāśrayakatadānukulyābhilāṣaviśeṣaḥ| itthambhūtā bhaktirityabhiprāyeṇaiva saccidānandaikarasatāyāṃ viśinaṣṭi śrutistasyāṃ bhagavadvaśyatāṃ ca darśayati vijñānaghanetyādinā bhaktirevainaṃ nayatītyādinā ca||*

Here again one needs faith, faith in the accounts of the lives of the *bhakti* saints that Dr. Kapoor draws his examples from, faith in the existence of *bhakti* as a kind of knowledge of relationship, and faith in his interpretation and retelling of the stories.

How is it then that Dr. Kapoor, who was such a careful thinker, appeals to equivocation in making his case for *bhakti* as science? My sense is that Dr. Kapoor is here not wearing the cap of a logician or philosopher. Instead he is practicing a kind of rhetoric, the art of persuasion. Thus, in addition to unpacking the idea of *bhakti* through his laws and the stories of the *bhakti* saints, he is playing the role of the rhetorician here, using the art to persuade his readers that they should become *bhaktas* or at least come to a higher appreciation of *bhakti*. The art of persuasive speaking is as old as history. Aristotle devotes a whole treatise to rhetoric as "the faculty of observing in any given case the available means of persuasion."[53] Note that rhetoric requires the observance or application of all available means of persuasion for the chosen audience, even the appropriate fallacies. Rhetoric's object is persuasion, not necessarily arrival at the truth. What one tries to persuade others of may indeed be true; certainly Dr. Kapoor's project was to make *his* truth as available and as attractive as possible to his readers.

Persuasion is achieved by three means, Aristotle tells us: the personal character of the speaker, putting the audience in a certain frame of mind and the "proof, or apparent proof, provided by the words of the speech itself."[54] Dr. Kapoor uses all three of these means very effectively in this work. His character as a learned and trustworthy scholar and philosopher contributes to his ability to persuade his readers, and his ability to evoke the sentiments of wonder and astonishment in them through his storytelling adds to the effectiveness of his presentation. Finally, the proof he adduces in the book which centers around the enthymeme, "*bhakti* is certain, therefore it is science,"[55] and the mounting inductive evidence of the sheer volume of stories from the lives of the saints greatly enhances the persuasive power of the text.

In the final analysis, those who want to be persuaded will be swept away by Dr. Kapoor's book. Those who do not want to be persuaded will

---

[53]Aristotle, *The Basic Works of Aristotle*, edited with an introduction by Richard McKeon, *Rhetorica*, 1.2, p. 1329. (New York: Random House, 1941)

[54]ibid.

[55]The whole syllogism from which the enthymeme draws its two parts would be: "everything certain is science; *bhakti* is certain; therefore, *bhakti* is science."

be charmed and maybe even tempted to persuasion. It is unfortunate that though Dr. Kapoor wrote this book in the 1970s and 1980s all the sources for his scientific understanding of the nature of reality were drawn from the 1920s and 1930s. It would have been wonderful to see a mind as rich as his reflect on more recent scientific theories about neural networks, string theory, parallel or holographic universes, non-locality, big bangs. quantum jitters, and so forth. In the end, though, all of this book's readers, persuaded and unpersuaded, will find they have learned a great deal about *bhakti* and will have passed their time reading dozens of delightful stories.

Experiences in *Bhakti*: the Science Celestial

What is *Bhakti*?

Bhakti cannot be easily defined because it is transcendental. Śāṇḍilya describes it as intense, loving attachment to God (*sā parānuraktir īśvare*).[1] Rūpa Gosvāmin describes it as the harmonious pursuit of Kṛṣṇa, unenveloped by *jñāna* (the quest for knowledge) and *karma* (ritual action) and uninterrupted by desire for anything else.[2] Nārada describes it as indescribable love of God and the most sublime of all human experiences,[3] on attaining which man craves for nothing else.[4] He is maddened with joy and delights in his own self.[5] He always swims in a ocean of nectar and is not drawn towards the enjoyments either of this world or of the next which are to him like the turbid waters of a muddy pool.[6]

Bhakti, a Function of the *Hlādinī-śakti*

These descriptions, however, give us only a general idea of the character of *bhakti*. They do not tell us what exactly it is. No one before Jīva Gosvāmin told us what it was. It was he who defined it for the first time as a function (*vṛtti*) of the *hlādinī-śakti* of Bhagavān (the Fortunate One, the Supreme Lord), the *śakti* (power) that causes bliss (*hlāda*). Bhagavān

[1]Śāṇḍilya, *Śāṇḍilya-bhakti-sūtra*, 2.
[2]Rūpa, *Bhakti-rasāmṛta-sindhu*, 1.1.9:

> *anyābhilāsitā-śūnyaṃ jñāna-karmādy-anāvṛtam*
> *ānukūlyena kṛṣṇānuśīlanaṃ bhaktir uttamā*

[3]*Nārada-bhakti-sūtra*, 2-3: *sā tv asmin parama-premarūpā (2); amṛta-svarūpā ca (3).*
[4]ibid., 5: *yat prāpya na kiñcid vāñchati na śocati na dveṣṭi na ramate notsāhī bhavati.*
[5]ibid., 6: *yaj jñātvā matto bhavati stabdho bhavaty ātmā-rāmo bhavati.*
[6]*Bhāgavata Purāṇa* (*Bhāg.*), 6.12.22.

places it in the hearts of his devotees so that they, as well as he, may be entranced.[7]

But how does one know that *bhakti* is the *śakti* of Bhagavān, not of the *jīva*? *Śruti* (the "heard" or revealed scriptures of India, also called the Vedas) says that Bhagavān is eternally unmanifest (*avyakta*). No one can see him without the help of his own *śakti*.[8] Only he can see or know him [Bhagavān] whom he [Bhagavān] himself chooses — *yam evaiṣa vṛṇute tena eṣa labhyaḥ*.[9] At the same time *śruti* says that *bhakti* alone takes the living being (*jīva*) to Bhagavān. *Bhakti* alone enables him to see him — *bhaktir eva enaṃ nayati, bhaktir eva enaṃ darśayati*.[10]

Bhakti, the Selfless, Loving Service of Bhagavān

Bhakti implies service. Selfless, loving service of the Lord is the essence of *bhakti*. Like the Kantian doctrine of the "categorical imperative" of duty for its own sake, *bhakti* implies a categorical imperative of service for its own sake. The devotee serves the Lord for the pleasure of the Lord, not for anything else.[11] But unlike the Kantian imperative, which is dry and exacting and an imposition from without, the categorical imperative of service to the Lord is the natural function of the soul and therefore pleasant and satisfying in itself. Though the devotee serves the Lord for the pleasure of the Lord, pleasure comes to him automatically. Such is the very nature of *bhakti*. But if the devotee's attitude of *bhakti* is tainted in the slightest degree with a concealed desire for his own pleasure, he is deprived to that extent of the supreme delight that comes from *śuddha* or pure *bhakti*. Even the pleasure that automatically comes to the devotee from an act of service is condemned by him, if it in any manner causes obstruction to service.

It is regrettable that the idea of service is not properly understood

[7] Jīva Gosvāmin, *Prīti-sandarbha*, 65.

[8] Cited in the *Bhagavat-sandarbha*, para. 45, as from the *Nārāyaṇādhyātma*:

> *nityāvyakto 'pi bhagavān īkṣyate nija-śaktitaḥ*
> *tām ṛte paramātmānaṃ kaḥ paśyetāmṛtaṃ prabhum*

[9] *Muṇḍaka Upaniṣad*, 3.2.3.

[10] *Māṭhara Śruti* cited by Baladeva Vidyābhūṣaṇa in his *Siddhānta-ratna*, 1.35.

[11] Bhāg., 6.12.22.

and appreciated by those who find it difficult to reconcile with their egos. They think that the path of *bhakti* is meant exclusively for persons who are intellectually weak and temperamentally submissive. They cannot understand that in the spiritual world, where love reigns supreme, to serve is to love and to love is to rule. In love self-sacrifice is self-realization and self-effacement is self-fulfillment. In love there is reciprocity. Each member of the relationship of love feels deficient without the other. Each wants to draw close to the other and to win the other by love and service. The Lord being the other member in the relationship of love in *bhakti*, he feels deficient without his devotee. He [Bhagavān] draws himself close to the *bhakta* to realize himself more fully through love and service to him. He derives greater pleasure in being controlled by his devotee than in controlling his devotee.[12]

Bhakti, a Spiritual Gravitational Force

Bhakti is a spiritual gravitational force that works at two ends. In our hearts it roots out all egoistic impulses that carry us away from the Lord and releases integrating forces that lead to complete surrender of all our faculties, so that knowledge, love, and will may act in complete harmony with the divine rhythm. In God it energizes his mercy and releases the forces of redemption which lead to the final integration of our being with Divine Will. This is confirmed by Kṛṣṇa's exhortation to Arjuna in which he asks him to surrender himself completely to his will and promises, on his doing so, to free him from all bondage and sin.[13] This is the principle of divine grace necessarily implied in *bhakti*.

It may be asked how the principle of divine grace can be reconciled with the transcendental and self-sufficient character of the Divine Being, who remains unaffected by *prakṛti* (material nature) and is without any desire or motive. The answer lies in the nature of *bhakti*. *Bhakti* is not something phenomenal. It is a function of the *hlādinī-śakti* (the power that causes bliss) of Bhagavān. It energizes, as we have seen, both Bhagavān and the devotee (*bhakta*). Like a lamp which reveals itself as well as other objects, the *hlādinī-śakti* of Bhagavān that he places in the heart of a pure devotee causes him, as well as the devotee, bliss. In fact, Bhagavān, the supreme relisher of bliss (*rasika-śekhara*), enjoys

[12]Bhāg., 9.4.64 and *Māṭhara Śruti*: *bhakti-vaśaḥ puruṣo bhaktir eva bhūyasī.*
[13]*Bhagavad-gītā.*, 18.66.

the bliss flowing from his *hlādinī-śakti* in the heart of his devotee (*śaktyānanda*) even more than he enjoys the bliss flowing from his own nature (*svarūpānanda*). On account of the gravitational force of the *hlādinī-śakti* the devotee is drawn towards Bhagavān and Bhagavān towards the devotee. Thus the devotee surrenders himself to Bhagavān and Bhagavān surrenders himself to the devotee. Grace is nothing but the surrender of Bhagavān to the devotee.

The whole of spiritual life is governed by the Law of Harmony. Love is the Law of Harmony in its highest form. Self-surrender on our part and mercy on the part of God are the manifestations of the Law of Harmony. In the *yoga* of self-surrender the soul strikes a divine chord and relishes an inner harmony which is of the highest order and a poise and equilibrium which is much more than intellectual.[14]

Bhakti, the Only Way to Attain Bhagavān

Bhakti is the only means to attain the supreme Lord. Śrī Kṛṣṇa said to Uddhava:

> *na sādhayati māṃ yogo na sāṅkhyaṃ dharma uddhava*
> *na svādhyāyas tapas tyāgo yathā bhaktir mamorjitā*
>
> It is not possible to attain me through *yoga*, *jñāna* (knowledge), the performance of duty, the study of the scriptures, penance, or renunciation in the way it is possible through strong *bhakti*.[15]

He also said:

> *sādhavo hṛdayaṃ mahyaṃ sādhūnāṃ hṛdayaṃ tv aham*
> *mad-anyat te na jānanti nāhaṃ tebhyo manāg api*
>
> The devotees are my heart and I am the heart of my devotees. They know nothing but me and I know nothing but them.[16]
>
> *ahaṃ bhakta-parādhīno hy asvatantra iva dvija*
> *sādhubhir grasta-hṛdayo bhaktair bhakta-jana-priyaḥ*

---

[14]After O. B. L. Kapoor, *The Philosophy and Religion of Śrī Caitanya*, 183-84.
[15]Bhāg., 11.14.20.
[16]ibid., 9.4.68.

Like one who has no freedom at all, I am completely under the control of my devotees as if they hold my heart in their hands.[17]

bhaktyā mām abhijānāti

By means of *bhakti* one knows me fully.[18]

Śrī Caitanya Mahāprabhu says that *jñāna*, the way of knowledge, *karma*, the way of action, and *yoga* do not lead to the same goal as *bhakti*.[19] *Jñāna* which consists of discrimination and contemplation leads to the realization of *nirviśeṣa* (formless and attributeless) *brahman* and the soul's immersion in it. *Yoga* which consists of the practice of *yama* (restraint), *niyama* (culture), *prāṇāyāma* (breath control), etc., leads to the realization of Paramātman (the highest or supreme self), a partial aspect of Bhagavān. *Karma*, which consists of the performance of *nitya* (compulsory) and *naimittika* (occasional) duties (rites), leads to the attainment of heaven for as long as the effect of the good deeds performed is not exhausted. But none of them leads to the attainment of Bhagavān.

Bhakti, the Essence of All Religions

It is important to note that even for the attainment of their respective goals, such as they are, *jñāna* and *yoga* have to depend on *bhakti*.[20] *Yoga* cannot even begin without *bhakti*, because it implies faith in Bhagavān whom the *yogī* aims at realizing in his partial aspect as Paramātman. No matter how long the *yogi* performs the yogic exercises and practices austerity, all his efforts will be set at nought if he lacks *bhakti*. Because the Paramātman is qualified (*saviśeṣa*) and we cannot realize him through *yoga* without *bhakti*, *yoga* is sometimes regarded as a kind of *bhakti* and is styled as *yoga-miśra-bhakti* (*bhakti* mixed with *yoga*) or *śānta-bhakti* (the *bhakti* of the pacified).

The necessity of *bhakti* for *jñāna* is recognized even by Śaṅkara. He says in his commentary on the *Gītā* that *jñāna-niṣṭhā* or fidelity to

[17]ibid., 9.4.63.

[18]*Bhagavad-gītā*, 18.55.

[19]Kṛṣṇa Dāsa Kavirāja, *Caitanya-caritāmṛta* (Cc), Madhya 20.121.

[20]ibid., Madhya, 22.14-5.

knowledge without which liberation is not possible is itself the result of *arcana-bhakti*, *bhakti* which consists of the ceremonial worship of the sacred images (the temple or home images of the gods).[21] Again in his commentary on the *Brahma-sūtra* he says that though liberation is the result of higher knowledge (*vidyā*), *bhakti* prepares the ground for higher knowledge by bringing the grace of God.[22]

The realization of *nirviśeṣa-brahman* (unqualified, impersonal *brahman*) through *jñāna* is also not permanent without *bhakti*. Śrī Caitanya speaks of two kinds of men who follow the *jñāna-mārga* (the path of knowledge) — those who do not have faith in Bhagavān and who seek to realize *nirviśeṣa-brahman* independently and those who have faith in him but desire to attain *mukti* (liberation).[23] The former attain release (*mukti*) and the state of immersion in *brahman* after a great deal of effort,[24] but there is every possibility of their again falling prey to *māyā*.[25] The latter attain the state of immersion in *brahman* more easily due to the grace of Bhagavān. Bhagavān lets them enjoy this state for some time but ultimately lifts them up to his own *dhāma* (abode) so that they may enjoy a state of contiguity with him, which is much more pleasurable than the state of immersion in *brahman*.

The *jīva* (living being) is an infinitesimal part of the *taṭastha-śakti* (marginal power) of Bhagavān who has come under the influence of *māyā*. The *jīva*'s power is limited. The power of *māyā*, as a *śakti* of Bhagavān, is unlimited. The *jīva* cannot, therefore, cross the bounds of *māyā* without the grace of God. *Jñāna*, *karma*, and *yoga*, involving independent efforts on the part of the *jīva* to overcome *māyā*, are of no avail. The only course open to the *jīva* is the path of *bhakti*. Kṛṣṇa himself says:

> It is difficult, indeed, to overcome my *māyā* independently of me. Only they can overcome it, who are sincerely devoted to me.[26]

Jñāna can, in a sense, lead to Bhagavān but not *jñāna* based on our limited understanding. Only *jñāna* which proceeds from the higher intelli-

---

[21]Śaṅkara, *Gītā-bhāṣya*, 7.56.

[22]Śaṅkara, *Śārīraka-bhāṣya*, 3.2.5.

[23]Cc., Madhya, 24.16

[24]Bg., 7.5.

[25]*Vāsanā-bhāṣya* on the *Yoga-sūtra*, cited in the *Bhakti-sandarbha*, para. 111: *jīvan-muktā api punar bandhanaṃ yānti karmabhiḥ*.

[26]Bg., 7.14.

gence granted by Śrī Kṛṣṇa to one who is sincerely devoted to him, or *jñāna* which is the product of *bhakti*, the *hlādinī-śakti* of Bhagavān, can dispel the clouds of ignorance and enable the *jīva* to attain Bhagavān.[27]

Thus, whatever be the path of religion, *bhakti* is essential for the realization of the goal. In fact, the path to realization is but one and that is the path of *bhakti*. This is the real teaching of the scriptures. Śrī Caitanya regards it (*bhakti*) as the very essence of the Vedas.[28] If people speak of many paths to realization, they do so because their intelligence is clouded by *māyā*.[29] The intelligences of different persons are differently conditioned by the three *guṇas* (qualities or strands) of *prakṛti* (material nature). Therefore they interpret the Vedas differently and speak of the paths to realization as more than one.[30] *Bhakti* is not only the essence of the Vedas but the essence of all religions.

---

[27] Bg., 10.10-11.

[28] Vṛndāvana Dāsa, *Caitanya-bhāgavata*, Madhya, 1.148 and 4.33.

[29] Bhāg., 11.14.9.

[30] Bhāg., 11.14.5-7.

Is *Bhakti* a Science?

It is important to know whether *bhakti* is a science or not, because the word 'science' has come to acquire a certain prestige. We do not easily believe a thing which is not a science. Unless we know that *bhakti* is a science, we would not be inclined to adopt it as an essential mode of our life and we would not make the readjustments in life in terms of self-surrender and self-discipline which it calls upon us to make.

The general belief is that *bhakti* is not a science because it is not based on observation and experiment, but on faith, unquestioning blind faith. It is true that *bhakti* starts with faith while science starts with doubt. *Bhakti* says: *saṃśayātmā vinaśyati* — one who doubts is doomed. Science says doubt is essential for the discovery of the truth.

The discoveries of *bhakti*, whatever they be, are restricted to the heart of the devotee. He cannot open his heart and show it to others, while the discoveries of science are open to all. The scientist can easily repeat his experiments and verify the results before everyone to prove the truth of the discoveries made by him, which the practitioner of *bhakti* cannot do.

Bhakti is Science in a Higher Sense

But *bhakti* is science in a higher sense for the very reason that it is based on faith. It is a science just because, fundamentally and primarily, it is not the result of any experiments conducted by man, but because it is based on revelation or truths revealed to us by God himself, which are even more sure and certain than the conclusions of science, based on observation and experiments made by man with his limited understanding and senses.

It may be objected that every science proceeds from self-evident principles, but *bhakti* proceeds from articles of faith which are not self-evident, since they are not admitted by all and therefore *bhakti* is not a science.

To this Thomas Aquinas replies:

> Sacred doctrine[1] is a science. We must bear in mind that there are two kinds of science. There are some which proceed from a principle known by the natural light of intellect, such as arithmetic and geometry. There are some which proceed from principles known by the light of a higher science. Thus the science of perspective proceeds from principles established by geometry and music from principles established by arithmetic. And in this way sacred doctrine is a science, because it proceeds from principles established by the light of a higher science, namely the science of God and the blessed. Hence just as the musician accepts on authority the principles taught him by the mathematician, so sacred science believes the principles revealed to it by God.
>
> The principles of any science are either in themselves self-evident or reducible to the knowledge of a higher science. And such, as we have said, are the principles of the sacred doctrine.[2]

Bhakti Properly Called a Science

Though, however, *bhakti* is primarily transcendental and divine in respect of its source and validity, there is nothing to preclude it from being treated as a science in the ordinary sense, for those who do not have faith in revelation. It can be shown to them that in the ordinary sense too it alone can properly be called a science.

In the ordinary sense science (from *scientia*, knowledge) means true and evident cognition, as distinct from opinion and belief, the truth of

---

[1]Religion or *bhakti*

[2]Thomas Aquinas, *Summa Theologica*, trans. by the Fathers of the English Dominican Province, rev. by D. J. Sullivan, First Part, Q. 1, Act 2. Published in the *Great Books of the Western World*, ed. R. M. Hutchins, vol. xix.

which is unconfirmed or unconfirmable. It is a body of certain knowledge about the nature of the things to which it relates and the laws that govern their behavior.

Therefore, in order to prove that *bhakti* is a science, we must ask two questions:

1. Is the knowledge acquired by *bhakti* true?

2. Are the laws of the science of *bhakti* certain?

We shall not only answer these questions, but compare them with the answers the so-called 'empirical sciences' have to give to similar questions in their respective spheres to show that *bhakti* alone is a science in the real sense of the term. The other sciences which started with the claim to be a science will now find themselves in a position in which, in spite of all their achievements, they are compelled to give up their claim, but continue to call themselves science, because of habit or because of the prestige attached to the word science.

Bhakti Alone Acquires Knowledge of God

Bhakti acquires knowledge of God. It claims that its knowledge is true. God exists. He is the creator and sustainer of the universe. He is omnipresent and he permeates every single object that exists. He can be seen by anyone who has the eyes to see — the spiritual eyes — which *bhakti* promises to give to anyone who would follow its way.

The [empirical] scientists do not agree. The nineteenth century scientists asserted dogmatically that God was an illusion. For them truth was always measurable. Everything could be brought within the scope of measurement by instruments and calculations based on them. What was called God or the Infinite was not a measureless something. It was only a question of time before it would become amenable to the scientific method.

Dogmatism is an intellectual disease and the scientist is not less prone to it than others, though he has less excuse for it, because he is supposed to be open-minded. Since his enquiry is limited to the empirical world he has no right to pronounce judgment upon the trans-empirical, which must always remain beyond his reach.

Twentieth century scientists are more open-minded. They are conscious of the limitations of the scientific method. Far from making any dogmatic assertions about God or anything pertaining to the sphere of reality which is beyond their reach, they frankly affirm that they are not able to say with certainty what even the things that fall within the scope of their enquiry really are.

Instead of saying that God is illusion, they seem to say that the world of science, the material world, is itself an illusion and what exists behind it is something which they cannot know, but which seems to support the view of the existence of a self-conscious Supreme Being that underlies everything.

Eddington, the noted astro-physicist, says that the scientist started with the object of discovering the exact nature of things with full confidence in his ability to do so, but "has got bogged in mathematical equations, which are only a partial account of something wider and have only the symbolic value of pointing to that something wider."[3]

It is specially the physicist's analysis of matter that has landed him in this predicament. He found that matter in the last analysis consisted of electrons. He began to study the electron. But the electron remained for him a mystery. Far from discovering its exact nature he could not even determine whether it was solid or liquid, for it sometimes behaved like a wave and sometimes like a particle. He had to assert that it was both wave and particle, in spite of the contradiction involved. He combined the two words 'wave' and 'particle' and said that it was a 'wavicle.' But 'wavicle' was only a name. It did not indicate what the electron really was. The only thing he could say about it with certainty was that it was nothing tangible. It was a 'process' or 'energy' which could be described only symbolically by means of algebraic equations.[4] Matter was thus reduced to an abstraction. It simply does not exist. It was an illusion. Not only matter, the entire panoramic world of sound and color, touch and taste, which fell within the scope of the scientist's enquiry was declared by him to be an illusion. Color, sound, touch were all sensations and the sensations existed in the mind, not in the world outside.

The position has been made very clear by the physiologist. He says with reference to color, for example, that it is not the object we see that

---

[3]Sir Arthur Eddington, *The Nature of the Physical World*, ?

[4]Sir James Jeans therefore says: "The universe cannot admit of material representation and the reason, I think, is that it has become a mere mental concept." Sir James Jeans, *The Mysterious Universe*, 167.

is colored. It is our physical apparatus that makes us see it as colored. Color exists as a sensation in the mind. It is superimposed by the mind on the object. What happens when we see a thing, for instance a brown table, is that the light of the sun or the lamp at night which falls upon the table is reflected back and meets the retina of our eye where it causes some chemical changes. The changes are carried in the form of a wave-like movement through the optic nerve to the back of the brain where they cause the sensation of color. The brown color of this table thus exists in the brain, not outside in the table. What exists outside is only the light wave.

The same is true of sound. Sound is physically a vibration in the air or a wave-motion. Vibrations originate in a sounding body. Focused by the outer ear they strike the outer membrane of the ear drum and set it vibrating. The vibrations are then communicated through the chain of bones, the inner membrane, the labyrinth and the auditory nerve to the brain, resulting finally in the sensation of sound.

According to the physiologist every single object as presented to us by our senses is a bundle of sensations — the sensations of sound, color, smell, touch, and taste. Since the sensations exist in the mind, the world, as presented by the senses, is mental and relative, not the world of things as they are in themselves.

Apart from the senses the other source of knowledge upon which the scientists depend is reason or understanding. But the knowledge provided by reason is also relative. Our understanding casts reality into its own mold before it presents it to us.

Eddington says: "We have found that where science has progressed the farthest, the mind has but regained from nature that which the mind has put into nature."[5]

In other words, the world of our experience is our own creation. It is what our senses and understanding make out of the stimuli that we receive from something outside. What that something is the scientist cannot say. The physicist ends by saying that it is 'energy.' But the energy, out of which he would derive the world, is as uncertain as matter. For when we ask for its production, we get only its supposed transformations, that is: sound, heat, light, etc. We do not find a pure energy in itself. Why? Because it is a conceptual creation useful only for conceptual purposes. Scientists have never perceived it. All that they have

[5]Sir Arthur Eddington, *The Nature of the Physical World,* ?

perceived of it are its appearances as sound, light, heat, etc.

> As a detachable reality it is still as uncatchable as matter. As a mathematical theory for practical purposes and as a calculator's symbol for technological purposes it takes a useful place, but it is still a supposition. It is supposed to work behind the universal movement, but it has never yet been exposed to view.[6]

The scientists, however, are compelled to say on account of the present state of scientific theory that something which underlies the world of our experience must be a conscious or spiritual reality. Eddington says in *The Nature of the Physical World*:

> If matter, in the sense of material substance, is eliminated from the world, spiritual existence is the only kind of model of reality that is left. This reality is likened to our conscious feeling, because now that we are convinced of the formal and symbolic character of entities of physics, there is nothing else to liken it to.[7]
>
> The idea of a universal Mind or Logos would be, I think, a fairly plausible inference from the present state of scientific theory; at least it is in harmony with it.[8]

J. S. Haldane says:

> The material world which has been taken for a world of blind mechanism is in reality a spiritual world. The truth is that not matter, not force, not any physical thing, Mind, Personality, is the central fact of the universe.[9]

The scientists have thus cleared the deck for the emergence of Mind, Personality, or God. But they can only infer God from the present state of scientific theory. They have no means to know him.

Science fails because it depends wholly on our ordinary understanding and senses which cloud our vision.

---

[6] P. Brunton, *The Wisdom of the Overself*, 14-5.

[7] Sir Arthur Eddington, *The Nature of the Physical World*, ?

[8] Sir Arthur Eddington, *The Nature of the Physical World*, 338.

[9] J. S. Haldane, *Mechanism, Life, and Personality: an examination of the mechanistic theory of life and mind.*, ? (New York: E. P. Dutton and Company, 1923 [Second Edition]) Perhaps this passage was removed or dramatically changed in the second edition to which I had access.

Bhakti Alone Purifies the Understanding and Senses

It is said that religion begins where science ends. *Bhakti* comes forward with the claim that it can show God. The *śruti* says: *bhaktir enaṃ darśayati* — *Bhakti* can show him face to face. Kṛṣṇa says in the *Bhāgavata:*

> Just as by the continuous application of an eye ointment, the eyes become clean and can see things which are difficult to see, the constant reading of the sacred texts relating to my sports or listening to them purifies the heart and the devotee is able to see me, who am otherwise too subtle to be seen.'[10]

Bhakti purifies and spiritualizes both sense and understanding and turns them into valid sources of knowledge. Thus the devotee can see Kṛṣṇa, while the ordinary person may see him and yet see not.[11] The washerman of Kaṃsa saw Kṛṣṇa, but was not blessed with the vision of his divine form because he lacked the essential quality of devotion.[12] An owl cannot see the rays of the sun even though he has eyes. So also it is not given to a man averse to God to perceive him.[13] But God can never hide himself from his devotee.[14]

Śrī Jīva Gosvāmin mentions two kinds of perception: *vaiduṣa*, which belongs to the wise who are purified by *bhakti* and *avaiduṣa* which belongs to those who are not purified. *Vaiduṣa* perception is free from all kinds of error; *avaiduṣa* is liable to err.

Similarly Śrī Caitanya distinguishes between lower and higher understanding. Lower understanding pertains to ordinary persons, higher to the sages.[15] The former, which is impure, does not help in spiritual

---

[10]Bhāg., 11.10.26:

yathā yathātmā parimṛjyate 'sau
mat-puṇya-gāthā-śravaṇābhidhānaiḥ
tathā tathā paśyati vastu sūkṣmaṃ
cakṣur yathaivāñjana-samprayuktam

[11]Vṛndāvana Dāsa, *Caitanya-bhāgavata*, 2.10.243.
[12]ibid., 248-51.
[13]ibid., 252-63.
[14]Cc., ādi 3.70.
[15]ibid., Madhya 24.121-122.

realization, but the latter, which is free from the influence of *prakṛti* or *māyā*, leads to the realization of God.[16] The five most important means of God-realization, namely, the service of the sacred images of Kṛṣṇa, the study of the *Bhāgavata*, the recitation of the holy name, the company of holy persons, and residing in Vṛndāvana are fruitful only in the case of persons who possess *subuddhi* or a higher, purified understanding.[17]

What happens when the heart and the understanding are purified is that there is an influx of *śuddha-sattva* (pure being) into the devotee's consciousness. *Śuddha-sattva* is the essence of the *sandhinī-śakti* or the power of God that is the foundational cause of all kinds of trans-natural existence, including the existence of God himself.[18] The influx of *śuddha-sattva* into the consciousness of the devotee results in such interpenetration of his personality by trans-natural existence that his perception and understanding, thought, feeling and will are wholly transformed and sublimated and he comes face to face with the Truth. The Truth is no more an external object of contemplation for him. He not only knows it, but he lives it. The Truth which always eludes the grasp of [empirical] science is thus, as the *Bhāgavata* says, within his grasp.[19]

The Laws of the Science of *Bhakti* Alone are Certain

Since the time of Galileo and Newton in the seventeenth century the world has been regarded as a big machine which worked according to mechanical laws. By the end of the nineteenth century even human beings began to be regarded as machines. It was supposed that their freedom of will was an illusion. Their behavior was strictly governed by the law of causation. It was the natural result of the mechanical causes present in the environment.

In the twentieth century there was a revolutionary development with the emergence of the electron on the scene. It was discovered that the atoms which till the end of the nineteenth century were regarded as the ultimate units of the physical world, which could not be further divided into smaller units, were but collections of millions of electrons.

[16] ibid., 123-24.
[17] ibid., 128-129.
[18] ibid., ādi 4.55.
[19] Bhāg., 9.4.63: *sādhubhir grasta-hṛdayo bhaktair bhakta-jana-priyaḥ*

The electrons were found to be wholly independent in their behavior. They were not governed by the mechanical causes which governed their collections, the objects of the physical world. The law of causation, upon which stood the entire structure of science, did not appear at all in the world of electrons.[20] The only law that determined their behavior was, in the words of Prof. Heisenberg, the Law of Indeterminacy.

Life would have been impossible, if we had to deal directly with electrons. Fortunately, the electrons remain behind the curtain. They are too small to be caught by our eyes or apprehended by us in any other manner. We have to deal with objects of which even the smallest is an aggregate of millions of electrons. Though in their individual capacity electrons are independent, in groups they behave according to the laws of science.

But the laws of science are not objective, for the electrons do not give up their independence even in groups. They are as independent as ever. They appear to behave uniformly, because, when they are in large groups, we do not attend to their independent functioning. We attend to the averages of their collective functioning. Sir James Jeans explains this by means of an example. He says that if we toss a coin into the air, we cannot say whether it will fall head upwards or tail upwards. If we toss one hundred or two hundred coins, we will not be able to say how many will come down heads up and how many tails up. But if we increase the number, the difference between those that fall heads up and those that fall tails up will, according to the mathematical law of averages, diminish. If we toss one million tons of coins, it is certain that half a million tons will fall heads upwards and half a million tons tails upwards. This will give us the impression of uniformity in the form of a law. There are in the smallest objects of the material world many more electrons than there are coins in one million tons of coins. Therefore, they appear to behave uniformly. The uniformity is not in the nature of things. The illusion of uniformity is created by the mathematical law of averages. Modern science removes that illusion.[21]

---

[20]"At any rate, the concept of strict causation finds no place in the universe which the new physics presents to us, with the result that this picture contains more room than did the old mechanical picture for life and consciousness to exist within the picture itself, together with the attributes which we commonly associate with them, such as free-will, and the capacity to make the universe in some small degree different by our presence." — Sir James Jeans, *The Mysterious Universe*, 35-6.

[21]ibid., 34: "In other words, when we are dealing with atoms and electrons in crowds, the mathematical law of averages imposes the determinism which physical laws have

Modern science regards its laws as probable, not necessary. Scientists do not know how the electrons come together and how long they will remain together. They may disintegrate at any time. The moment they do so, the illusion of the uniformity of nature and its objects will end. The sun rises every day, but whether it will rise tomorrow or not the scientist cannot say with certainty. But the probability of its rising tomorrow is so great that we need not lose our sleep over it.

The situation in the science of *bhakti* with regard to the certainty of laws seems, at first sight, to be the same as in the natural sciences. *Bhakti* is concerned with the *jīva* (living being) and *Bhagavān* (the Supreme Person). Each is free in its behavior like the electron. The laws of uniformity and causation do not bind them. But as uniformity is introduced in nature by the law of averages, uniformity is introduced in the realm of *bhakti* by the law of love. In love neither Bhagavān nor the devotee has any freedom of his own. Each is bound by the love of the other. The *Caitanya-caritāmṛta* says:

> *kṛṣṇere nācāya prema bhaktere nācāya*
> *āpane nācaye, tine nāce eka-thāñi*
>
> Love makes Kṛṣṇa dance. It makes the devotee dance. It dances itself. The three dance together.[22]

The devotee says like Mīrā: "Thy will be done. I am completely sold out to thee."[23]

Kṛṣṇa says: *ahaṃ bhakta-parādhīno hy asvatantra iva dvija*, "I am subservient to my devotee. I am like one who has no freedom at all."[24]

The *Caitanya-caritāmṛta* says:

> *yadyapi īśvara tumi parama-svatantra*
> *tathāpi svabhāve hao prema-paratantra*

---

failed to provide."

[22]Cc., Antya 18.17.

[23]Mīrābai:

> *merī unkī prīti purāṇī*
> *un vinā pala na rahāūñ*
> *jahān baiṭhāve tahān hi*
> *baiṭhūñ bece to bikha jāūñ*

[24]Bhāg., 9.4.63.

> Although as the great lord you are completely free in all respects, yet you are by nature completely subjugated and determined by love.[25]

The difference between science and *bhakti*, however, is that while in science the uniformity introduced by the law of averages is an illusion, in *bhakti* the uniformity introduced by the law of love, is real. The laws of *bhakti* are not probable, but certain.

[25] Cc., Madhya 12.26.

The Laws of *Bhakti*

Every science has its laws. So has *bhakti*. The fundamental laws of *bhakti* may be enunciated as follows:

1. The law of gravitation.
2. The law of reciprocation.
3. The law of subjugation.
4. The law of unification.

We have said the laws of the science of *bhakti*, unlike the laws of the other sciences, are divine in origin. We shall locate the divine origin of each law and explain it.

The Law of Gravitation

The law of gravitation in *bhakti* may be stated as follows:

Bhakti attracts Kṛṣṇa.

We have already stated that *bhakti* has a gravitational force on account of which Kṛṣṇa is automatically attracted to the devotee. Śrī Rūpa Gosvāmin says in his *Bhakti-rasāmṛta-sindhu* that *bhakti* is *śrīkṛṣṇākarṣaṇī*[1] or that which attracts Kṛṣṇa. The attraction of *bhakti* in the heart of the devotee to Kṛṣṇa is so great that He is compelled to say:

anuvrajāmy ahaṃ nityaṃ pūyeyety aṅghri-reṇubhiḥ[2]

---

[1]Rūpa Gosvāmin, *Bhakti-rasāmṛta-sindhu*, 1.1.42.
[2]Bhāg., 11.14.16.

> I always trail behind my devotee so that I may be purified by the dust of his feet.

We have also said that *bhakti* is not something phenomenal, but transcendental. It is the *hlādinī-śakti* of Kṛṣṇa himself, which he plants in the heart of a devotee who sincerely wants to serve him. How is it that Kṛṣṇa is attracted by his own *hlādinī-śakti* planted in the heart of his devotee? It is because it provides greater happiness to him when it resides in the heart of his devotee. Śrī Jīva Gosvāmin explains this with reference to the example of the flute and the flute player. The flute-player is capable of producing a whistling sound by blowing air out of his mouth. But when he blows the same air into the flute and makes it pass through its different holes, it produces a sound that is so melodious that the flutist himself is charmed by it. Similarly the *hlādinī-śakti* has a relish of its own which is sweet beyond description when it resides in Kṛṣṇa, but its relish increases a thousandfold when it is implanted in the heart of the devotee. The devotees have a passionate desire to serve Kṛṣṇa according to their different *bhāvas* (sentiments). The *hlādinī-śakti* mixes with the different *bhāvas* of his devotees and acquires a variegation (*vaicitrya*) which is so astonishingly sweet that even Kṛṣṇa is charmed by it. Therefore, he always implants his *hlādinī-śakti* in the hearts of his devotees who want to serve him.

As soon as the desire to serve Kṛṣṇa arises in the heart of the devotee, it generates a corresponding desire in him to relish that service. The more passionate is the devotee's desire the more it makes him restless to accept his service and enjoy it. The enjoyment of a food is commensurate with the intensity of the appetite. Similarly, Kṛṣṇa's enjoyment of the loving service of the devotee is commensurate with the intensity of his appetite for it and the intensity of his appetite depends on the intensity of the devotee's *bhakti* or keenness to serve him.[3]

But how can Kṛṣṇa accept the devotee's service if he remains on the transcendental plane and the devotee on the phenomenal plane and if he has no need for his service and feels neither thirst nor hunger nor heat nor cold? The attraction of the devotee's loving service makes him come down to his level in the form of the Śrī Vigraha or the holy image and accept all its limitations. He suffers hunger and thirst and heat and cold to enjoy the food and drink and the clothes lovingly offered to him by the devotee.

---

[3] Rūpa Gosvāmin, *Padyāvalī*, 10.

Does he merely pretend to? No, the *līlā-śakti* (the sport-effecting power) *yoga-māyā* contrives to make him forget his divinity and actually feel hunger and thirst and all else that is felt by the devotee himself to enable him to fulfill his desire for relishing the devotee's service. Numerous instances of the image's dependence on the devotee for the fulfillment of his wants can be pointed out. We shall cite only a few.

Examples

Bāla-gopāla served by Kṛṣṇa Prema

Kṛṣṇa Prema (Ronald Nixon) used to serve as *pūjāri* (ritual priest) in the temple of Bāla Gopāla (Child Kṛṣṇa), the deity of his guru Yaśodā Mā in Mirtolā, a village in the Himalayas. One night while Kṛṣṇa Prema was asleep, he heard someone calling "Dādā, Dādā (Big Brother, Big Brother)!" With a start he got up and looked around but could not see anyone. Thinking that it was just an illusion he lay down and closed his eyes. But again he heard the same sweet call: "Dādā!" This time it was clear that the call came from inside the temple.

But there was no one inside the temple except the sacred image (*ṭhākura*). Could it, therefore, be the call of the image? He went nearer to the temple and heard, "Dādā, I am feeling cold. The window is open"

A shiver passed through the spine of Kṛṣṇa Prema. He opened the door of the temple, went inside, and saw that the window was really open. He closed the window and carefully covered the body of Bāla Gopāla with a quilt. While doing so he said: "Ṭhākura [Lord], you also feel cold?"

A stream of tears flowed from the eyes of the image. Kṛṣṇa Prema was petrified. Why did the image weep? He wept because Kṛṣṇa Prema's remark touched the innermost core of his heart. For he was not the great lord, the creator and destroyer of the universe, but a child, who depended entirely upon the loving care of his *dādā* (elder brother) and who wanted to love and be loved, to enjoy the most intimate, sweet, and loving relationship between himself and his *dādā*. Had not his *dādā* thrown cold water upon his hopes and aspirations by his question? It betrayed an attitude of mind not congenial to such an intimate relationship.[4]

[4]Kapoor, *Saints of Vraja*, 302.

Śrī Kṛṣṇa Candramā served by Lālā Bābu

Lālā Bābu (Kṛṣṇa Candra Sinha) was born in 1775 with a silver spoon in his mouth. His grandfather Gaṅgā Govinda Sinha was the owner of a large estate and the Governor of Bihar and Bengal when Warren Hastings was the Governor General of India. Lālā Bābu also became the Governor of Orissa. Besides that, he inherited all the extensive property of his grandfather. He was the richest and most respectable man of Eastern India at this time. But a spark of *bhakti* always disturbed his mind. He renounced everything and went to Vṛndāvana.

He built the magnificent temple in Vṛndāvana now known as Lālā Bābu's temple. In the temple he installed the beautiful images of Rādhā and Kṛṣṇa. The image of Śrī Kṛṣṇa was named Śrī Kṛṣṇa Candramā. After the *prāṇa-pratiṣṭhā*[5] ceremony was duly performed one day in the month of January, a strange thought came to his mind.

He asked the *pūjārī* to keep a small lump of butter on the head of Śrī Kṛṣṇa Candramā. The *pūjārī* looked at Lālā Bābu with surprise. Lālā Bābu said: "Yes, yes, do as I say. I want to see whether the deity is really alive after the *prāṇa-pratiṣṭhā*. If alive, the butter should melt on account of the heat of his head.

The *pūjārī* had to obey. A small quantity of butter was placed on the head of Śrī Kṛṣṇa Candramā. After some time the butter actually melted and began to flow down his cheeks. The *pūjārī* and the other devotees present in the temple cried aloud with tears of joy in their eyes: "Śrī Kṛṣṇa Candramā kī Jaya!" Lālā Bābu was so overwhelmed with *bhāva* (feeling) that he fell unconscious on the ground.[6]

Gaura and Nitāi Served by Pisi Mā Gosvāminī (Candraśaśī)

Pisī Mā Gosvāminī used to serve Gaura and Nitāi in the temple of Gaura and Nitāi near Bana-khaṇḍī Mahādeva in Vṛndāvana. She belonged to the famous Mukhopādhyāya family, the landlords of Delagrāma in the district of Nadiyā. She had motherly affection (*vātsalya*) for the images. For their sake she renounced family and all her wealth at the age of twenty and came to live in Vṛndāvana with them (Gaura and Nitāi). Pisī Mā served Gaura and Nitāi like her children with great devotion. When she became a hundred years old it was not possible for her to

[5] A ritual performed at the time of the installation of an image to bring it to life.
[6] Kapoor, ibid., 112.

serve them any more. She then deputed Śrīpāda Gopeśvara Gosvāmin, a descendent of Nityānanda Prabhu, for the service. Gopeśvara Gosvāmin was a devoted person. His attitude (*bhāva*) towards Gaura and Nitāi was of the friendly type (*sakhya*).

But Gaura and Nitāi, who were accustomed to the motherly affection and service of Pisī Mā, perhaps could not adjust themselves immediately to the friendly affection and service of Gopeśvara Gosvāmin. Pisī Mā used to bathe them in warm water in the winter. Gopeśvara Gosvāmin bathed them in cold water. So they caught colds.

Pisī Mā then lived in a room on the first floor of the temple and seldom came down. But whenever anything happened which caused displeasure or discomfort to Gaura and Nitāi, its vibrations touched her heart. She came to know about the colds they were suffering from. She came down to see them. She saw that their eyes were red and phlegm was flowing from their noses. She wiped the phlegm away with the corner of her *sārī*. She also touched their bodies and found that they were running temperatures. She then called Gopeśvara Gosvāmin in and said: "What have you done? You have bathed my children in cold water and now their noses are running." As she said this, she showed him the corner of her *sārī* which as stained with Gaura and Nitāi's phlegm. Gopeśvara did not believe her. Pisī Mā in anger held the other corner of her *sārī* near Gaura's nose and said: "Bābā, sneeze a bit." Gaura sneezed. Again phlegm came out of his nose and the temple was filled with its supernatural aroma. Gopeśvara Gosvāmin fell down at Pisī Mā's feet in penitence.[7]

The Law of Reciprocation

The law of reciprocation is stated thus:

*The Lord reciprocates the feelings (*bhāva*) of his devotee.*

It is based on Kṛṣṇa's own declaration:

ye yathā māṃ prapadyante tāṃs tathaiva bhajāmy aham[8]

I reciprocate the *bhāva* or devotional feelings of my devotee.

---

[7]ibid., 138.

[8]*Bhagavad-gītā.*, 4.11.

Brahmā says in his hymn to Kṛṣṇa:

> *yad yad dhiyā ta urugāya vibhāvayanti*
> *tat tad vapuḥ praṇayase sad-anugrahāya*[9]
>
> Through whatever conceit your devotees worship you, you appear to them in that form to show your grace to the good.

The different kinds of devotional feeling that devotees may have in their relationship with Bhagavān are classified into five broad categories of *rasa*. Those are *śānta* (quietistic devotion), *dāsya* (devotion as servitude or faithfulness), *sakhya* (devotion as friendship), *vātsalya* (devotion as parental feeling), and *mādhurya* (devotion as the sweet sentiment between lover and beloved). The *hlādinī-śakti* or the divine power of bliss itself is a harmonious combination of all these *rasas*, but it is reflected differently in different devotees according to the differences of their loving attitudes towards Kṛṣṇa. It is just like the way the same rain water tastes different when it mixes with different terrestrial objects. In milk it tastes sweet, in *āmalakī*[10] sour, in some vegetables salty, in pepper pungent, in *gulañca*[11] bitter and in *harītakī*[12] astringent. The examples or ideals of *śānta-rasa*[13] are Sanaka, Sanātana, Sananda, and Sanatkumāra; the examples of *dāsya-rasa* are Raktaka, Patraka, Madhukaṇṭha. The examples of *sakhya-rasa* are Śrīdāma, Sudāma, Subala, and others; the examples of *vātsalya-rasa* are Nanda, Yaśodā, Vasudeva, and Devakī; the examples of *madhura-rasa* are the *gopīs* (cowherd girls) of Vṛndāvana and the wives of Kṛṣṇa in Dvārakā. The devotee enjoys the type of *rasa* that characterizes his devotion. But Kṛṣṇa as *rasika-śekhara* or the supreme enjoyer of *rasa* enjoys all the different types of *rasa* through them.

The devotional attitudes giving rise to different kinds of *rasa* have, however, been only broadly classified into *śānta*, *dāsya*, *sakhya*, *vātsalya*, and *madhura*. There is in fact no limit to the kinds of devotional attitude. Each of those five kinds of attitude may again be divided into

[9]Bhāg., 3.9.11.

[10]Emblic myrobalan.

[11]A climbing plant used in Ayurvedic medicine.

[12]Yellow myrobalan.

[13]These are the names of individuals from the Purāṇas and other *bhakti* literature who are generally thought of as examples of the various forms of *bhakti-rasa*. Dr. Kapoor seems to have in mind here a specific passage from the *Caitanya-caritāmṛta* of Kṛṣṇa Dāsa Kavirāja (Madhya 19.162-164).

different kinds. Besides, a particular attitude may be a mixture of several attitudes.

Kṛṣṇa responds to each devotee according to his attitude. The attitude of the *śānta bhakta* does not involve any kind of personal relationship with Kṛṣṇa. His attitude is entirely dominated by the *aiśvarya* (godly power and opulence) of Kṛṣṇa. Therefore Kṛṣṇa appears to him as his partial manifestation, Nārāyaṇa in Vaikuṇṭha. He has no place in Vraja, where the devotees have some kind of personal relationship with Kṛṣṇa. The *śānta bhakta* thinks that he belongs to Nārāyaṇa, not that Nārāyaṇa belongs to him. The dominance of *aiśvarya* in his orientation makes it impossible for him to think in such terms. But the devotees of Vraja not only think that they belong to Kṛṣṇa, but also that Kṛṣṇa belongs to them as their master, friend, child or beloved. Therefore Kṛṣṇa appears to them as such. The devotees in Vraja serve Kṛṣṇa in the manner natural to their type of feeling. But the *śānta-bhakta* does not serve Nārāyaṇa. He enjoys visions of him and contiguity with him, but not intimacy with him.

It follows from the law of reciprocation that Kṛṣṇa has as many forms as the devotional attitudes of the devotees and in each form his figure, attitude and divine sport (*līlā*) correspond to the attitude of the devotee. In other words each devotee's Kṛṣṇa is his own and no one else's. This is proven by some of his divine sports. In the circle dance (*rāsa-līlā*), in which he danced with each cowherd girl, each girl felt that he was dancing with her and no one else. Similarly when Nārada went to Dvārakā to see him, he was surprised to see that he was engaged in a different kind of activity in the palace of each one of the sixteen thousand, one hundred and eight queens.

The *śruti* says: *eko 'pi san bahudhā vibhāti,*[14] "though he is one, he appears as many."

Śrī Caitanya Mahāprabhu emphasized that though he appears in infinite forms, his identity remains the same.[15] In the *Bhāgavata* he is called *bahu-mūrtyaika-mūrtikam,*[16] "you who have one form in many forms."

The *vaidurya* jewel[17] appears to be a different color from each direction it is gazed upon. It has all those colors in it. Similarly, Śrī Bhagavān has all those different forms in his sacred image. In the case of a par-

---

[14]*Gopāla-tāpanī,* 1.5.

[15]Kṛṣṇa Dāsa Kavirāja, ibid., Madhya 20.144: *ananta-prakāśa kṛṣṇer nāhiñ mūrti-bheda*

[16]Bhāg., 10.40.7.

[17]A precious and rare stone.

ticular devotee he manifests the particular form that corresponds to the devotee's feelings.

This seems to involve a contradiction. Kṛṣṇa has a two-armed form in Vraja where he appears as the son of Nanda and Yaśodā and a four-armed form in Mathurā and Dvārakā where he appears as the son of Vasudeva and Devakī. If he is the same deity how can he be two-armed as well as four-armed?

But Bhagavān is above contradictions. The law of contradiction is a form of our understanding. It does not apply to Bhagavān, who transcends our understanding. Bhagavān is Bhagavān or the all-perfect being only because he has the inconceivable power of resolving all contradictions. This is evident from the *śrutis* which describe him as *aṇor aṇīyān mahato mahīyān* — smaller than the smallest and bigger than the biggest[18] — and *āsīno dūraṃ vrajati śayāno yāti sarvatra* — he travels far while sitting and moves about everywhere while sleeping.[19] Śrī Jīva proves Bhagavān's inconceivable power of holding contradictory attributes together by quoting the *Brahma-sūtra* text: *ātmani caivaṃ vicitrāś ca hi*, "And thus in the self [the Lord] are many variegated things,"[20] and other *śrutis*.[21]

If the finite mind cannot understand the inconceivable power of the infinite to hold contradictions together, it is but natural. If it could, the infinite would not be infinite, just as the sun would not be the sun, if it could be illumined by a lamp.

It is therefore that the *Kena Upaniṣad* says:

> *yasyāmatam tasya mataṃ mataṃ yasya na veda saḥ*
> *avijñātaṃ vijānatāṃ vijñātam avijānatām*[22]
>
> To one who thinks he does not know [Bhagavān], he is known. One who thinks he knows does not know. [He is] unknown to those who know and known to those who do not know.

And Brahmā, the creator of the universe, says:

---

[18] *Śvetāśvatara Upaniṣad*, 3.2.20.

[19] *Kāṭhaka Śruti*, 1.2.21.

[20] *Brahma-sūtra.*, 2.1.28.

[21] Śrī Jīva, *Sarvasaṃvādinī*, 143-4. Jīva Gosvāmin, *Sarva-saṃvādinī*, edited by Rasikamohana Śarmā (Vidyābhūṣaṇa), (Calcutta: Sanskrit Sahitya Parishad, 1933).

[22] *Kena Upaniṣad*, 2.3.

jānanta eva jānantu kiṃ bahūktyā na me prabho
manaso vapuṣo vāco vaibhavaṃ tava gocaraḥ[23]

My Lord! Let those who say they know you go ahead and say so. I cannot say I know you. My mind, body, and words fail to grasp you.

The Law of Subjugation

The law of subjugation states:

Bhakti subjugates God.

Śruti says: *bhakti-vaśaḥ puruṣo bhaktir eva bhūyasī*, "*Bhakti* subjugates the Lord; *bhakti* is great."[24]

Kṛṣṇa says in the *Bhāgavata*: *ahaṃ bhakta-parādhīno hy asvatantra iva dvija*, "I am completely subjugated by my devotee like one who has no freedom at all."[25]

In the *Padma Purāṇa* he says: *mad-bhaktānāṃ vinodārthaṃ karomi vividhāḥ kriyāḥ*, "[I am so under the subjection of my devotees that] I perform different kinds of sport to please them. [I have nothing else to do]."[26]

To please his devotees the Lord forgets his *aiśvarya* (lordliness) and serves them in various ways. It is the love of his devotees that makes him do so.[27] In the soothing and enchanting light of their love his *aiśvarya* shrinks and his *mādhurya* (sweetness) bursts and blooms in the same manner in which in the light of the full moon the ocean swells and the tides flow. The love of Yaśodā makes the all-powerful and all-pervading Kṛṣṇa allow himself to be tied by her: the love of Nanda makes him carry his shoes on his head; the love of his friends and companions makes him carry them on his shoulders; the love of the wives of the sages makes him beg for food at their doors; the love of the cowherd women of Vraja makes him roll at their feet.[28]

---

[23] Bhāg., 10.14.38.

[24] *Māṭhara Śruti.*

[25] Bhāg., 9.4.63.

[26] Cited in Sanātana Gosvāmin's *Bṛhad-vaiṣṇava-toṣaṇī* on Bhāg., 10.1.2.

[27] Cc., 3.18.17: *kṛṣṇere nācāya prema bhaktere nācāya.*

[28] Kapoor, *The Philosophy and Religion of Śrī Caitanya*, 123.

It is no exaggeration to say that Kṛṣṇa rolls at the feet of the cowherd women. This is illustrated by an anecdote from the life of the great poet and devotee Jayadeva. Jayadeva was writing his famous poem the *Gīta-govinda*, describing Kṛṣṇa's efforts to appease the wrath (*māna*) of Rādhā. In the last part of the last line of the poem he wanted to write: *dehi me pada-pallavam udāram*, "place your lotus feet on my head." But he began to hesitate. He left the last part of the line blank and went to bathe in the Ganges. All the time he was thinking whether it was proper to make Kṛṣṇa stoop so low. When he returned he was surprised to find that the blank was already filled in by someone in the very manner he had hesitated over. The words *dehi me pada-pallavam udāram* were clearly inscribed in it. He asked his wife who had done it. She replied: "Why who else could? Did you not come back immediately after you had gone out and then leave again after filling in the gap?"

Jayadeva stood stunned. His hairs stood on end and tears flowed from his eyes. He understood that it was Kṛṣṇa himself who had come in his guise and filled in the gap.[29]

The reason why the love of the devotee makes Kṛṣṇa forget his *aiśvarya* and behave like one subservient to his devotee is inherent in Kṛṣṇa's very nature as *rasa*. *Rasa* is concentrated transcendental bliss or *ānanda*. The ultimate source of *ānanda* is Kṛṣṇa's *svarūpa-śakti* (his internal or inherent power), or more correctly Kṛṣṇa's *svarūpa-śakti* dominated by its own partial aspect, the *hlādinī-śakti* (the bliss-giving power, *hlādinī-pradhānā svarūpa-śakti*). Therefore, the *ānanda* enjoyed by Kṛṣṇa is also caused by the *hlādinī-śakti*. There are broadly speaking two categories of *ānanda* which the *svarūpa-śakti* provides for Kṛṣṇa — *svarūpānanda* and *svarūpa-śaktyānanda*. The *hlādinī-śakti* residing in Kṛṣṇa enables him to enjoy his *svarūpānanda*, or the bliss inherent in his own self. The *hlādinī-śakti* residing in the heart of a devotee desirous of serving Kṛṣṇa assumes the form of *kṛṣṇa-prīti* or love for Kṛṣṇa, which is much more enjoyable to Kṛṣṇa than his own *svarūpānanda*. The *ānanda* which the *hlādinī-śakti* enables Kṛṣṇa to derive from the love of his devotees is called *svarūpa-śakty ānanda*.[30]

Svarūpa-śakty ānanda is of two kinds: *aiśvaryānanda* (godly-joy) and *mānasānanda* (mental-joy). The dominant aspect of a devotee's real-

[29]Nābhāji, *Bhakta-māla*, 170. In the translation of Nābhājī into Bengali by Lāladāsa (17th cent.), edited by Avināśacandra Mukhopādhyāya, this story is found on pages 164-5. (Kalikātā: Akṣaya Lāibrerī, 1360 [1954])

[30]Śrī Jīva Gosvāmin, *Prīti-sandarbha*, para 62.

ization of Kṛṣṇa may either be his knowledge of the *aiśvarya* (divine power) of Kṛṣṇa or the *mādhurya* (sweetness) of Kṛṣṇa. The *kṛṣṇa-prīti* (love for Kṛṣṇa) of devotees in whom the knowledge of his *aiśvarya* predominates is naturally *prīti* mixed with knowledge of *aiśvarya* (*aiśvarya-jñāna-miśra-prīti*). The *ānanda* that Kṛṣṇa derives from such love is *aiśvaryānanda*. Love is always shy before knowledge of Kṛṣṇa's divine power. It flows freely when that knowledge is absent. The more knowledge of Kṛṣṇa's divine power the less the intensity of love.

Love dominated by knowledge of divine power is enjoyable because there is also an element of sweetness in it. But it is not as enjoyable as love dominated by knowledge of sweetness. There are also devotees who have no knowledge of Kṛṣṇa's divine power at all. Kṛṣṇa to them is not the great lord, the creator, sustainer, and destroyer of the universe, but only a sweet and loving person, having all the human wants and weaknesses. Their love is relished by Kṛṣṇa more than anything else. The joy Kṛṣṇa derives from it is called *mānasānanda*.

In Vaikuṇṭha, love is entirely dominated by *aiśvarya*. In Dvārakā and Mathurā it is governed by *mādhurya* more than by *aiśvarya*. But in Gokula and Vṛndāvana it is entirely governed by *mādhurya*. This does not mean that in Gokula and Vṛndāvana there is no *aiśvarya*. Both *aiśvarya* and *mādhurya* are present here in their most perfect forms. But *mādhurya* has the natural tendency to cover and conceal *aiśvarya*. *Mādhurya* in its highest form envelops *aiśvarya* completely. Therefore, in Vaikuṇṭha Bhagavān enjoys *aiśvaryānanda*. In Dvārakā and Mathurā he enjoys *aiśvaryānanda* mixed with *mādhurya*. But in Gokula and Vṛndāvana he enjoys *mānasānanda*. In Vṛndāvana *mādhurya* is intensified because of the birth and other sports of Kṛṣṇa which are not manifested in Gokula. Therefore the joy of Vṛndāvana is superior to the joy of Gokula.

The highest manifestation of love is possible only when neither Bhagavān nor his devotee is conscious of Bhagavān's divinity. This is possible only in Vraja where Bhagavān has the two-armed human form (*narākṛti*). In Vraja, though in reality *para-brahman* (the highest *brahman*), he has the natural conceit of being an ordinary human being. Though in reality eternal and without beginning or birth, he thinks of himself as the son of Nanda and Yaśodā and of Nanda and Yaśodā as his parents. The style of his dress, which is like that of a cowherd boy, the peacock feather, which he is fond of wearing as his crown, and his flute are all the emblems of his *mādhurya*, not of his *aiśvarya*. Therefore the flavor of love in Vraja is the highest flavor (*rasa*) and the sport of Vraja the highest sport.[31]

How much the Lord enjoys the love that is completely free of awareness of his divine power (*aiśvarya*) and unrestricted by feelings of reverence towards him is evident from his exhortation to Prahlāda as described in the *Hari-bhakti-sudhodaya*. The Lord says to Prahlāda:

> Because you think of me as the great Lord, you have feelings of fear and reverence towards me. Give up that fear and reverence. I do not like that kind of attitude. Let your love for me be free from all constraints. Although I am *pūrṇa-kāma* (all my desires are fulfilled), I crave the love of my devotees who are wholly free in their talk and behavior towards me. I am attracted by their love; in it I find new pleasure. Though eternally free, I am eternally a captive in their hands.[32]

It is Kṛṣṇa's craving for *mānasānanda* that makes him subservient to his devotee. Indeed, subservience to the devotee is an essential condition for the generation of *mānasānanda*. Therefore, on account of his very nature as *rasa* (delightful flavor) he is eternally a slave of the devotees who love him. He is above everything but not above love. He controls everything but is controlled by love.

The Law of Unification

The law of unification states:

> Bhakti *unites the* bhakta *(devotee) and Bhagavān*

The *Bhagavad-gītā* says:

> By means of *bhakti* my devotee knows me fully and is united with me.[33]

---

[31] Kṛṣṇa Dāsa Kavirāja, Cc., Madhya 21.83:

śrīkṛṣṇer yateko khelā, sarvottama nara-līlā
naravapu tāhār svarūpa
gopeśvara veṇukara, navakiśora naṭavara
naralīlā anurūpa

[32] *Hari-bhakti-sudhodaya*, 14.27-30.

[33] *Bhagavad-gītā.*, 18.55:

And then again:

> I am the same towards everyone. I neither hate nor love anyone. But towards my devotees who love me, my love is so intense that I feel they are in me and I in them.[34]

The *Bhāgavata* says:

> Bhagavān soon enters the heart of one who always narrates or listens to stories about Kṛṣṇa with faith.[35]

And,

> My devotees are my heart and I am theirs.[36]

In the *Brahma-vaivarta Purāṇa*, Kṛṣṇa says to the cowherd girls:

> You are the same as I. There is no difference between you and me. I am your life breath and you are like my life-breath to me.[37]

The state of identity between *bhakta* and Bhagavān is called *viśrambha*. It is a state of highly intensified love. This identity, however, is not like the identity of the living being with Brahman in *sāyujya-mukti* (the liberation of union).[38] This is an identity in which the difference between

---

bhaktyā mām abhijānāti yāvān yaś cāsmi tattvataḥ
tato māṃ tattvato jñātvā viśate tad-anantaram

[34]ibid., 9.29:

samo 'haṃ sarva-bhūteṣu
na me dveṣyo 'sti na priyaḥ
ye bhajanti tu māṃ bhaktyā
mayi te teṣu cāpy aham

[35]Bhāg., 2.8.4:

śṛṇvataḥ śraddhayā nityaṃ gṛṇataś ca sva-ceṣṭitam
kālena nātidīrgheṇa bhagavān viśate hṛdi

[36]ibid., 9.4.68:

sādhavo hṛdaym mahyaṃ sādhūnāṃ hṛdayaṃ tvaham

[37]*Brahma-vaivarta Purāṇa, Kṛṣṇa-janma-khaṇḍa*, 27.237:

yathāhaṃ ca tathā yūyaṃ nāhaṃ bhedaḥ śrutau śrutaḥ
prāṇo 'haṃ caiva yuṣmākaṃ yūyaṃ prāṇā mama prabhoḥ

[38]Śrī Rūpa Gosvāmin, *Ujjvala-nīlamaṇi*, 14.110 (or 14.78 in the Murshidabad edition).

āśraya (lover) and *viṣaya* (the beloved) is not obliterated; otherwise love itself would not be possible. Rādhā describes this state of identity to her friend as follows:

> In that state neither is Kṛṣṇa the lover nor I the beloved. Our love is so enchanting and absorbing that because of the intensity of our desire to bring happiness to each other, each forgets not only his separate identity, but identity itself. The consciousness of the lover and the beloved is gone. What remains is only the consciousness of love, which seems to experience itself. It is as if love melts each of us and makes us one.[39]

Śrī Jīva says that the identity (in the state of *viśrambha*) is like the identity between fire and a piece of iron. When the iron is immersed in fire, it becomes fire, but though it becomes fire its separate identity as iron is not lost.

Viśvanātha Cakravartin describes *viśrambha* as the total absence of feelings of difference or hesitation. Those feelings of difference or hesitation are natural when one's beloved is regarded as having an identity separate from one's own and a general attitude of reverence, however unimportant and undetectable, characterizes one's behavior towards that person. This absence of feelings of difference is possible only when the *prāṇa* (life-force, breath), *manas* (mind), *buddhi* (intellect), and *deha* (body), etc. of the lover are regarded as identical with their counterparts in the beloved.[40] In other words, when the lover's concern for the life of the beloved is the same as his concern for his own life, when he feels that what appears as pleasure and pain to him also appears as pleasure and pain to his beloved, and when he thinks that what appears as true or false, good or bad or indifferent to him appears as true or false, good or bad or indifferent to his beloved. On account of this feeling of identity the lover does not hesitate to do with the beloved what he does not hesitate to do with himself. For example, he does not hesitate to touch any part of the body of the beloved with his foot, just as he does

---

[39]Kṛṣṇa Dāsa Kavirāja, Cc., Madhya 8.153:

> *nā so ramaṇa nā hām ramaṇī*
> *duhuñ mana manobhāva peśala jāni*

[40]Viśvanātha Cakravartin, *ānanda-candrikā* on Un., 14.78 (110).

not hesitate to touch any part of his own body with it. This is why the playmates of Kṛṣṇa do not have any hesitation in riding on his shoulders or offering him things to eat which they have themselves already partly eaten.

Because in unification Bhagavān feels the pleasure and pain of his devotee as his own, a subsidiary law that follows the law of unification as its corollary is the law of protection according to which Bhagavān says:

> For my devotees who have completely surrendered themselves to me, who depend only on me and who think only of me and no one else, I look after their needs and welfare.[41]

[41] *Bhagavad-gītā.*, 9.22:

> *ananyāś cintayanto māṃ ye janāḥ paryupāsate*
> *teṣāṃ nityābhiyuktānāṃ yoga-kṣemaṃ vahāmy aham*

Are the Laws of the Science of *Bhakti* Verifiable?

The Laws of *Bhakti* Do Not Need Verification Because They Are Based on Revelation

Verification is a characteristic of what is normally called a science. Since in *bhakti* or religion knowledge is derived primarily from revelation, most people do not regard it as a science. But as we have already said *bhakti* is a science just because it is based on revelation or truths revealed by God. The truths revealed by God do not need verification.

The laws of *bhakti* constitute knowledge of God. As such, they are necessary and eternal, unlike the truths discovered by what is ordinarily called science, which are probable and hold good only for the time being. The scientist has unsaid many things he said in the past and may unsay tomorrow what he says today. Even the most fundamental propositions of science have undergone change. We have seen how the existence of matter, which was regarded as foundational to science, is now regarded as illusion. Matter was regarded as the basic reality and consciousness was regarded as its by-product. But consciousness is now regarded as basic and matter in the form of energy is regarded as derivative from consciousness. Space and time were regarded as absolute by science, but they are now regarded as relative. Einstein's Theory of Relativity has proved that there is no definitive length of space or time. The same lengths indicated by the same measuring instruments can vary widely in different planets and galaxies according to their varying velocities.

The Validity of Revelation is Vindicated by Modern Science

Indeed the world-view of modern science seems to come closer to the world-view of the *Bhāgavata* religion, based on revelation. The concept of energy or *śakti* is as prominent in the *Bhāgavata* religion as in modern science. The material world, according to the *Bhāgavata* religion, as according to modern science, does not exist in its own right. It is the manifestation of energy or *śakti*. Space and time also are according to the *Bhāgavata* religion relative, not absolute. This is apparent from the *Brahma-mohana-līlā* (the sport of confusing Brahmā), described in the *Bhāgavata Purāṇa*.[1] Brahmā stole the calves and the cowherd boys who had gone to the forest with Kṛṣṇa for pasturing. He hid them somewhere and went back to Brahmaloka.[2] The period between his disappearance and reappearance on the scene was equal to only a few moments according to the time-scale in Brahmaloka, but it was one year in Vraja.[3] During the whole of this period Kṛṣṇa himself functioned as an exact replica of each of the calves and cowherd boys to conceal the theft and to cause bewilderment in Brahmā.

What is most surprising is that the electron, which according to modern science, is more like consciousness than anything phenomenal, is said to behave very much like Brahman. *Śruti* describes the inconceivable power of Brahman by saying that it goes far and wide without moving.[4] Similarly modern science says that the electron goes from one place to another without crossing the intermediate points, in violation of all the laws of mechanics.

This thoroughly vindicates the validity of revelation as a source of knowledge as against the method of science which is based on observation and experiment. It is because *bhakti* is based on revelation that it can make the absolute claim that its propositions are true, not that they are probably true, which is the best claim that science based on

[1] Bhāg., 10.13.
[2] The planet of Brahmā.
[3] Bhāg., 10.13.40.
[4] *Kaṭha Upaniṣad*, 1.2.21: *āsīno dūraṃ vrajati śayāno yāti sarvataḥ*

observation and experiment can make. If we ignore this claim of *bhakti* and try to construct a science of *bhakti* on the basis of observation and experiment, we shall not have a science of *bhakti* in the real sense, but only in the sense that its propositions, though not wholly true, are as true as the propositions of the other sciences based on observation and experiment.

Though Not Needed, the Laws of *Bhakti* Can Be Verified

Though, however, the truths of *bhakti* stand on the solid ground of revelation and do not need verification, that does not mean that they are not verifiable for those who do not have faith in revelation. They can be experientially verified, if by experience we do not mean only sense experience, but experience of any kind. Obviously, they cannot be empirically verified because they are trans-empirical. They can be verified only in spiritual experience.

But the experiments in the science of *bhakti* are not as easy as in the empirical sciences. The biggest difficulty is that the experiments here relate to the self, not to the world outside. In *bhakti* the individual is his own laboratory. In the experiments of the empirical sciences changes have to be made in things other than the self. In *bhakti* changes have to be made within one's own self. It is not as easy to make changes in the self as it is to make changes in other things.

Some of the experiments in the empirical sciences too are not easy to make. They are too technical to be performed or even to be understood by the layman. He has to depend on the experts for the verification of the truths sought to be proved by them. The laws of the empirical sciences are the result of generalization from the results obtained by experts in the experiments made by them. *Bhakti* also can be treated as an experiential science on the basis of generalizations made from the results obtained by experts or advanced devotees in the experiments made by them.

Another difficulty in the experiments of *bhakti* as an experimental science is the element of grace involved in its experiments. In *bhakti* or, broadly speaking, in religion, the grace of God is regarded as essential for the successful conclusion of an experiment. All religions, whether

Hinduism, Christianity or Islam, admit the necessity of the grace of God for the experience of God. The *Kaṭha Upaniṣad* says: "By him the *ātman* [Supreme Being] is attained whom it chooses."[5] Christ says: "You did not chose me, but I chose you ... "[6] Our love of God such as it is "resides not in our showing any love for God, but in his showing love for us first."[7] Even an Advaitic (non-dualistic) work like the *Viveka-cūḍāmaṇi* mentions the need for the grace of God at least twice.

The devotee's dependence on the grace of God seems at first sight to introduce an external factor into *bhakti*, over which there is no control, and therefore an element of uncertainty into the experiments of *bhakti* which nullifies its character as an experimental science. But the grace or mercy of God is not an extraneous factor in *bhakti*. It is *prema-bhakti* (holy love) itself functioning through God. God does not control it but is himself controlled by it. Kṛṣṇa Dāsa Kavirāja explains this in relation to Mahāprabhu's mercy on Mahārājā Prataparudra.[8] Mahāprabhu was adamant on not allowing the Mahārājā to see him, but he found his mercy more powerful than him. It prevailed upon him to such an extent that he was compelled to give the Mahārājā a loving embrace in a state of unawareness.[9]

We have seen that in the realm of *prema-bhakti* it is not God who rules but holy love (*prema*). To repeat the lines of the *Caitanya-caritāmṛta* quoted above: "It is love that makes both Bhagavān and the *bhakta* dance. It dances itself and the three dance together."[10] The grace of God is nothing but God dancing as love makes him dance. It is but an aspect of the law of reciprocation in *bhakti*. Reciprocation implies self-surrender in the loving service of God on the part of the *bhakta* and grace on the part of Bhagavān.

Grace is no doubt independent of practice (*sādhanā*). It is causeless

---

[5]ibid., 1.2.23.

[6]Gospel of John, 15.16.

[7]ibid., 4.10. This seems to be a based on a faulty translation of the text from John. The text in versions I checked reads something like: Jesus answered her: "If you knew what God can give you, and who just said to you 'Give me a drink,' you would ask him and he would give you lively, life-giving water." Robert W. Funk, et al, *The Five Gospels: The Search for the Authentic Words of Jesus* (New York: Macmillan Publishing Company, 1993) The idea of dependence on the grace of God, however, is present in both versions. [Ed.]

[8]The king of Orissa during Śrī Caitanya's residence in Puri.

[9]Kṛṣṇa Dāsa Kavirāja, *Caitanya-caritāmṛta*, Madhya 14.16.

[10]ibid., Antya 18.17.

as far as the efforts of the practitioner (*sādhaka*) to win the grace of God are concerned. But it is not causeless so far as love is concerned. It is the warmth of the love of the *bhakta* that causes the heart of Bhagavān to melt and flow in the form of grace. If this were not so Bhagavān's subjugation by the *bhakta* would have no meaning.

It will be our effort in the following chapters to show how the truths or the fundamental laws of the science of *bhakti* have been verified by numerous devotees whose lives themselves have been for us like prolonged experiments in *bhakti*. Before, however, we proceed to do so, we must once again reiterate that *bhakti* is primarily a transcendental science and it claims validity for its laws because they are divine with respect to their source. It is experiential science only for those who do not have faith in their divine origin. Since their number is not small, it is mainly for them that we shall try to show how the laws of the science of *bhakti* stand verified by the experiences of the devoted practitioners.

Verification of the Law of Gravitation

Bhakti attracts Kṛṣṇa in more ways than one. He is attracted:

1. by the *bhakti* in the heart of the devotee.
2. by the offerings lovingly made by the devotee.
3. by the devotee's dance, *kīrtana*, and talks about him.

Bhakti in the Hearts of the Devotees

How much Kṛṣṇa is attracted by the *bhakti* of his devotees is obvious from what he said about them to Durvāsas and Uddhava. He said to Durvāsas:

> *nāham ātmānam āśāse mad-bhaktaiḥ sādhubhir vinā*
> *śriyaṃ cātyantikīṃ brahman yeṣāṃ gatir ahaṃ parā*
>
> I always desire the company of my devotees who completely surrender themselves to me and depend entirely on me. Without them my own self, my wife Lakṣmī, and all my possessions are nought to me.[1]

He said to Uddhava:

> *na tathā me priyatama ātma-yonir na śaṅkaraḥ*
> *na ca saṅkarṣaṇo na śrīr naivātmā ca yathā bhavān*

[1] Bhāg., 9.4.64.

> You are more dear to me than any one else. [My son] Brahmā, [my incarnation] Śaṅkara, [my brother] Saṅkarṣaṇa [Balarāma], [my wife] Lakṣmī and even my own self are not as dear to me as you.[2]

The law of gravitation in *bhakti* in this form stands verified by the examples of hundreds of devotees of which we shall mention a few.

Examples

Lokanātha Gosvāmin and Ṭhākura Rādhāvinoda

Lokanātha Gosvāmin, one of the closest companions of Śrī Caitanya Mahāprabhu, was requested by him to go to Vraja and rediscover the holy places connected with the divine acts (*līlā*) of Śrī Kṛṣṇa. Vraja-Vṛndāvana was at that time covered with forests. He went from forest to forest in quest of any signs of the holy places. While he was engaged in this task, his mind was set on Kṛṣṇa and his *līlā*. He always shed tears in remembrance of them.

Once when he was staying under a *tamāla* tree, near Kiśorī-kuṇḍa, a pond in the forest of Chatravana, he thought, if he had with him Śrī Kṛṣṇa himself in the form of his image, he could serve and please him so that he might help him in his exploration. The moment he thought that, Kṛṣṇa felt attracted towards him and became restless to receive his service. He thought of a clever device to reach him immediately in the form of the sacred image. He went to him in the guise of a tribesman with his own image and said: "Mahārāja! This is my Ṭhākura (sacred image) Rādhāvinoda. I have been serving him since long. Now I have become old and cannot serve anymore. I am leaving him with you. I shall be happy if you kindly serve him."

This was like a bolt from the blue to Lokanātha. The benign Lord had responded to his desire and come to him of his own accord. Tears of love and gratitude streamed out of his eyes. He took the image, held it close to his heart and was for some time lost within himself. On regaining outer consciousness he looked all around for the man who had brought the image, but he was nowhere to be seen. Who was he and where had he gone after doing him that great favor? The thought was plaguing

[2] ibid., 11.14.15.

his mind, when Rādhāvinoda smiled and said: "Who could bring me? I have brought myself. I was lying in the Kiśorī-kuṇḍa nearby. Since you desired eagerly to serve me, I have come. I have been forcibly drawn by your love. I could not resist the temptation of enjoying your service. I am very hungry. Give me something to eat."[3]

Rādhāvinoda remained with Lokanātha till the end. Lokanātha made a bag from the fibre of some plant, in which he carried him wherever he went. Rādhāvinoda felt happier in it than even in his celestial abode in Vaikuṇṭha or Goloka.[4] It is said that he was of great assistance to Lokanātha in discovering the sites where his own acts took place. Nārāyaṇa Bhaṭṭa Gosvāmin writes in his *Vraja-bhakti-vilāsa* that Lokanātha discovered as many as three hundred and thirty-three forests and places connected with the divine acts of Śrī Kṛṣṇa.[5]

Sanātana Gosvāmin and Ṭhākura Madanagopāla

Sanātana Gosvāmin was also entrusted by Mahāprabhu with the task of rediscovery and revival of holy Vṛndāvana. He lived in Vṛndāvana at Aditya-tilā on the bank of the Yamunā, but went to Mathurā for alms-food (*madhukarī*), because at that time there was no human habitation in Vṛndāvana. Once he happened to go to the house of Dāmodara Caube. There he saw the beautiful image of Madanagopāla. The image stole his heart. He was lost in a trance of deep feeling. He wished he had the opportunity of offering his loving service to Madanagopāla. He tried to suppress the desire. What was the use of entertaining a desire which could not be fulfilled? It was futile to think that the Caube family would give away their Ṭhākura to him. Even if they did, how and from where would he get all the means to serve him as well as the Caube family did?

But it was not possible to suppress the desire. The more he tried to suppress it the stronger it grew. All the time, whether he was asleep or awake or in meditation, the image of Madanagopāla emerged in his mind and made him restless. He went to Caube's house again and again on the pretext of begging for alms-food and returned after visiting Madanagopāla.

---

[3]Narahari Cakravarti, *Bhakti-ratnākara*, 1.331-333.

[4]ibid., 1.334-338.

[5]This work is regarded as authentic because it was written in 1553 C.E. when Rūpa and Sanātana were present and it was approved by them.

We have said that the law of gravitation in *bhakti* functions at two ends. It draws the *bhakta* to Bhagavān and Bhagavān to the *bhakta*. Madanagopāla could not remain unaffected by the seed of feeling (*bhāva*) and *bhakti* that had sprouted in the heart of Sanātana. The day the desire for the loving service of Madanagopāla arose in the mind of Sanātana it evoked a similar desire in the mind of Madanagopāla. He also began to long for the loving service of Sanātana. As Sanātana's attraction towards him increased his attraction towards Sanātana also increased.

There was no end to Sanātana's happiness and astonishment, when one day Caube's wife, who had motherly affection for Madanagopāla and served him lovingly, said to him in a sorrowful mood and with tears coursing down from her eyes. "Bābā! From today you have to accept the responsibility of the service of Madanagopāla. Gopāla has now grown up and become restive and unmanageable. He does not want to remain under the protection of his mother. He asked me in a dream yesterday night to give him to you. I have also become old and forgetful and cannot serve him well. It is in his interest that I entrust him to someone who can serve him well and with affection."

Fortune smiled on Sanātana. He returned to his hut with the treasure of his heart.

Sanātana built another hut of straw near his own in which he installed Madanagopāla. For his offerings of food he had to depend on begging for alms-food. From the flour he got by begging, he prepared *bāti* by kneading flour, rolling it into balls and baking the balls on a fire. He offered the *bāti* to Madanagopāla with a saltless and spiceless vegetable dish, prepared from leaves he collected in the forest. Madanagopāla kept on somehow swallowing this fare for a few days, hesitating to complain about it. But he could not carry it on indefinitely. One day he said to Sanātana in a dream: "Sanātana, I find it difficult to swallow your balls of flour with leaves boiled without salt. I have to push them down my throat forcibly. How long can I continue to do so? Why not give me some salt along with these?"

Tears of love trickled down from the eyes of Sanātana. In utter helplessness he said in all humility with folded hands: "Prabhu! You know that your humble servant is a recluse without any wherewithal for your service. You ask for salt today. Tomorrow you may ask for molasses and then for a meal fit for royalty. How shall I manage? I have been enjoined by Mahāprabhu to follow the ideal of a Vaiṣṇava renunciant who is supposed not to ask for anything from anyone and to remain content with whatever he gets in alms. You know that in begging for alms people give flour but no salt."

Did Madanagopāla feel humiliated? Did he think of going back to the house of Dāmodara Caube where he got better things to eat? No. Greedy persons do not mind humiliation. His greed for the loving service of Sanātana was so great that he preferred to suffer humiliation and eat the poor and saltless food Sanātana gave rather than leave him. For him the love behind the food Sanātana offered was more precious than the food itself.

Gaurāṅga Dāsa Bābā and Girirāja

Bhagavān's greed and attraction for the loving service of the devotee is so great that he sometimes goes out of his way to ask for it himself even at the risk of suffering denial and humiliation. This is what happened once with Gaurāṅga Dāsa Bābā.

One night Gaurāṅga Dāsa Bābā saw in a dream that from a place near his hut in Govardhana an image of Girirāja was calling him, saying: "Take me to your hut. I long for your service." Next morning, when he went to that place, he saw that some persons had started digging a well. On digging only two or three feet, a beautiful image of Girirāja appeared. Gaurāṅga Dāsa Bābā recognized it as the same image that had appeared to him in the dream. He at once lifted and hugged it and brought it to his hut.

He began to serve Giridhārī as well as he could. But how could the company of ascetic Gaurāṅga Dāsa and luxurious Giridhārī last long? Gaurāṅga Dāsa never begged for anything from anyone except for alms-food. But there was no end to the demands of Giridhārī. He would ask for silken clothes, a golden flute, a golden crown, the choicest scents, fruits, sweets and what not. Gaurāṅga Dāsa had to spend all his time in catering to his needs. He had hardly any time left for meditating on the divine play which his teaching guru, Siddha Jagadīśa Dāsa Bābā, had asked him to do.

In this plight he went to Jagadīśa Dāsa Bābājī in Vṛndāvana and reporting everything to him, said: "Now you tell me whether I should obey you and spend all my time meditating on divine play or obey Giridhārī and spend my time in fulfilling his never-ending demands?"

Jagadīśa Dāsa Bābā said: "With folded hands you express to Giridhārī your inability to serve him and go and leave him on Govardhana hill. You should yourself follow the path of abstinence and private worship shown by Śrī Rūpa and Sanātana."

Gaurāṅga Dāsa Bābā did as advised. Poor Giridhāri was deprived of Gaurāṅga Dāsa's much coveted company and service.

Jaikṛṣṇa Dāsa Bābā and Śrī Kṛṣṇa

Jaikṛṣṇa Dāsa Bābājī was engaged in private worship (*bhajana*) on the bank of Vimalā-kuṇḍa in Kāmyavana. The seed of *bhakti* had already sprouted in his heart. As soon as it blossomed into flower, Kṛṣṇa, like a black bee, was attracted by its fragrance. He came in the guise of a cowherd with his cows and other cowherds and knocked at Bābā's door to ask for water, as if he had gotten thirsty while pasturing the cows in the forest. Bābā did not open his door because he thought some boys had come who often disturbed him during his worship.

Kṛṣṇa shouted: "Bābā, we are thirsty. Give us water." But Bābā would not listen.

Kṛṣṇa shouted again: "O Bengali Bābā! What worship do you do? What is the use of your worship if it makes you so heartless? Why can't you come out and give us water? Don't you know it is an offense to turn away thirsty persons from one's door?"

Bābā came out with a stick in hand. But as soon as he came out, he was surprised to see so many boys, each surpassing the other in beauty and luster and so many beautiful cows such as he had never seen before. His anger subsided. He asked a boy with a peacock feather on his crown: "Lad, where do you live?"

"I live in Nandagaon," replied the boy.

"What is your name?"

"My name is Kanhaiyā."

Bābā then asked another boy, standing by his side: "What is your name?"

"Baladau,"[6] replied the other boy.

Kanhaiyā said: "Bābā, first give us water. Our throats are parched."

Bābā did not have any cups or glasses. Therefore Kṛṣṇa cupped his hands and Bābā poured water into them from his water pot. The water, instead of falling into his hands fell like a stream on the ground, but

[6]Kanhaiyā and Baladau are nicknames of Kṛṣṇa and his brother Balarāma. These are also very common names of boys in Vraja.

neither the devotee nor Bhagavān was aware of it. Each was absorbed in looking at the other like one enchanted, for such was the spell of love between them. Was Kṛṣṇa really thirsty? No. He was thirsty for the ambrosia of the flavor of *bhakti* flowing from the eyes of his devotee and was drinking it in to his heart's content through the cups of his eyes. He became aware of the fruitless exercise of drinking water only when the other boys laughed and clapped their hands when they saw it.

After Kanhaiyā had drunk water, he said: "Look Bābā! We come here from a long distance every day and return thirsty. We shall now be coming to you everyday. Kindly also keep some refreshments for us."

Bābā said: "No, no. Don't come to disturb me in my worship again!"

Immediately he went into his hut and shut the door. But there was something so mysteriously attractive in the boys that he had hardly shut the door, when he was tempted to open it again to have another look at them. To his surprise he found that the cowherd boys and the cows had all disappeared. Where could they have gone in a moment? Was it all a dream or hallucination? But no, it was not a dream, for he was fully awake. It was not a hallucination for it was even more vivid and real than anything he had seen before. Besides, the sweet and somewhat maddening fragrance of the bodies of the cowherds still filled the air and the water that had spilled on the ground was also there.

Suddenly the awareness dawned on him that Kanhaiyā and Baladau were Kṛṣṇa and Balarāma themselves whom he had been worshiping. A current of deep feeling (*bhāva*) ran through his body. Tears flowed from his eyes. He was overwhelmed with joy and emotion at the thought that he had seen Kṛṣṇa, the treasure of his heart and soul of his soul. But the joy turned into grief as soon as he remembered that he had, like a fool, asked Kṛṣṇa not to come again. But was Kṛṣṇa to be dissuaded from coming, because the devotee had asked him not to come? Was his attraction for the devotee so faint and flimsy? No. He was all the more determined to come. He again appeared before Bābā with an enchanting smile on his face and said: "Bābā! I shall come to you tomorrow and never leave again." He said this and disappeared.

The next day Vṛndā, the presiding deity of Vṛndāvana, came to Bābā in the form of an old woman with an image of Gopāla and said: "Bābā! I have become old. I cannot serve Gopāla. I am leaving him with you so that you may kindly serve him."

Bābā realized that Kṛṣṇa had come to him as promised in the form of Gopāla. Kṛṣṇa remained with him in this form to enjoy his loving service till the end.[7]

Gauracaraṇa Dāsa Bābā and Dāujī (Balarāma)

Gauracaraṇa Dāsa Bābā was born in the family of Lokanātha Gosvāmin. At a very early age he took initiation from Siddha Śrī Caitanya Dāsa Bābā of Navadvīpa. After remaining in the service of his guru for a long time he requested permission to go to see holy Vraja and return. His guru was a great realized being (*siddha-mahātmā*). He knew that Kṛṣṇa and Balarāma would be so attracted by his *bhakti* that they would not let him come back. He said: “Go, but will you be able to return? Having gone there you may find yourself in the love-trap of Kṛṣṇa and Balarāma and they may not let you come back.”

Gauracaraṇa said: “No, Gurudeva. You may rest assured that I will return quickly after circumambulating Vraja.”

Gauracaraṇa went to Vraja. He performed the circumambulation (*parikramā*) of Vraja. At the conclusion of his ambulation he went to Mahāvana and viewed Dāujī (the image of Balarāma). He decided to pass the night there and set out for Navadvīpa at dawn. During the night, when he was asleep, Dāujī called him by name and said: “Look, Gauracaraṇa, you are very dear to me. So remain here and do private worship (*bhajana*) in the cave you see over there.”

Gauracaraṇa said: “No, I will not stay here. I will go back to Navadvīpa as I have promised my guru.”

“I will not let you go,” said Dāujī with a playful smile on his lips.

Gauracaraṇa found himself in a predicament. He did not know whether he should keep his promise to his guru or obey Dāujī. After reflecting on it for a while he said: “No, no. I shall go. I shall leave this very moment.”

Even as Gauracaraṇa said this, he sprang up, slung his bag over his shoulder and set out for Navadvīpa. It was midnight. Darkness prevailed over all. Yet he was marching as fast as he could. As he was marching the words of his guru rang in his ears: “Go, but will you be able to return?” And sometimes the words of Dāujī came to him: “I will not let you go.” The smiling face of Dāujī seemed to draw him

[7]This story is found in Haridāsa Dāsa’s *Śrī Śrī Gauḍīya Vaiṣṇava Jīvanī*, Vol. 2, 131-3. [Ed.]

back. But he was pushing forward with long strides. Every now and again he looked back to see if Dāujī was chasing him from behind. He was determined to stop and rest for a while only when he had crossed the perimeter of Vraja. When he had gone a long distance he thought surely he was out of Vraja. But as the day dawned he was surprised to see where he was. He exclaimed: "Oh! Have I, like a fool, only been going around and around Baladevakuṇḍa[8] all night? The illusion must have been created by Dāujī."

The words of his *gurudeva* came true. Gauracaraṇa realized that it was not possible for him to get out of the love-trap of Dāujī. He began to live and practice private worship in the cave pointed out by Dāujī. It is said that Dāujī at times went to his cave and gave him butter and sugar-candy.[9]

Śrī Rādhāramaṇacaraṇa Dāsa Deva

Sacred images (*ṭhākuras*) sometimes seem to vie with each other in accepting the service of a devotee. Śrī Rādhāramaṇa Caraṇa Dāsa Deva of Purī was one such devotee. He was known also as Barha Bābā (Big Bābā), and his uncommon *bhakti* attracted to him a number of images. He went about freely from place to place along with his disciples dancing, singing the name of the Lord, and arousing the *māyā*-bound living beings of Kali from their slumber. He did not want to be tied down to one place by undertaking responsibility for the service of a particular image in a monastery (*maṭha*) or *āśrama*. But Śrī Rādhākānta, the image of the Jhānjapītā Maṭha of Purī, founded by Śrī Sevā Dāsa at the instance of Śrī Narottama Dāsa Ṭhākura,[10] longed for his service. He managed to create circumstances under which Barha Bābā was compelled to take charge of the Jhānjapītā Maṭha as well as the responsibility of his service.[11]

After some time there was a sweet disturbance in his heart and he came to know that four other images also longed for his service. He

---

[8]A pond in Mahāvana named after Baladeva.

[9]This story is taken from Haridāsa Dāsa's *Śrī Śrī Gauḍīya Vaiṣṇava Jīvanī*, Vol. 2, 78-79. [Ed.]

[10]The only disciple of Śrī Lokanātha Gosvāmin.

[11]*Carita-sudhā* (Hindi), 244-247. *Life of Love* (English Adaptation of the *Carita-sudhā* by O.B.L. Kapoor), 227-231.

called Lakṣmaṇa Mahārāṇa, a carpenter, and asked him to make a beautiful and spacious altar (*siṃhāsana*) for the images.

Lakṣmaṇa said: "I will make it. I think an altar big enough for Rādhā and Rādhākānta will do."

Bābā said: "No. Four other deities are expected soon. The altar should be big enough to accommodate the guests along with Rādhā and Rādhākānta."[12]

The altar was made. After Rādhā and Rādhākānta were seated on it one of the disciples of Śrī Rādhāramaṇa Caraṇa Dāsa Bābājī asked, "When will those other images arrive?"

Bābājī: "They will arrive in ten or twelve days."

Disciple: "Where will they come from?"

Bābājī: "Two of them will come from Haridvāra and two from Calcutta."

Disciple: "Are all the four images of Rādhā and Govinda?"

Bābājī: "The two images from Haridvāra are Rādhā and Govinda. They are called Rādhā and Rādhāvinoda.[13] Those from Calcutta are Gaura and Nitāi."

One day Bābā wrote a letter to Jogen Bābu, one of his disciples in Calcutta, asking him to send as soon as possible a *hukkā*[14] with a long pipe and the best type of tobacco that might be available. A disciple standing by was reading the letter. He asked: "What will you do with the *hukkā* and the tobacco?" Bābā replied, "The image who is coming from Haridvāra smokes a *hukkā*."

The *hukkā* and tobacco soon arrived. The stage was set for the right royal reception of the royal guests.

---

[12]Śrī Rādhāramaṇa Caraṇa Dāsa Bābājī could have built separate altars for the guests. Why did he make a spacious altar in which they could all be accommodated together? Was it because the guests were so near and dear to Rādhā and Rādhākānta that they wanted them to stay as close to them as possible? So it was. Rādhā and Rādhāvinoda are but different manifestations of Rādhā and Rādhākānta (Kṛṣṇa, the husband of Rādhā). Nitai is the combined manifestation of Balarāma and Anaṅga Mañjarī. Balarāma is non-different from Kṛṣṇa, and Anaṅga Mañjarī, the younger sister of Rādhā, is non-different from Rādhā. Anaṅga Mañjarī is inseparable from Rādhā even at the time of her most esoteric play with Kṛṣṇa, in which her service is indispensable (see the *Anaṅga-mañjarī-sampuṭikā*). Besides, Nitai as the image of service, the very embodiment of service, is inseparable from Rādhā and Kṛṣṇa (*Caitanya-bhāgavata*). He is always with them in the form of their clothes, ornaments, bed, altar, and everything else that is directly or indirectly used in their service, including even the air they breathe (*Caitanaya-caritāmṛta*, ādi 5.9.)

[13]Different images of Rādhā and Kṛṣṇa are called by different names.

[14]A water-filtered pipe used in India.

The guests were already on the move. They had been lying for some time underground in a hill near Haridvāra. One day Vinodajī appeared in a dream before a *brahmacārī* devotee and said: "We are lying under the ground over there. Dig us up and serve us." The *brahmacārī* obeyed. He served them with devotion for some time. Then Vinoda said to him in a dream: "Brahmacārī, we are happy with your service. But we yearn passionately for the service of Bābā Rādhāramaṇa Caraṇa Dāsa of the Jhānjapītā Maṭha in Purī. Take us to him." The *brahmacārī* was sorry to hear this. But he had to obey.

One morning he arrived at the Jhānjapītā Maṭha with the images. Bābā, who was already anxiously waiting for them, began to dance in joy. He bathed and duly installed them by the side of Rādhākānta. The *brahmācārī* told him the whole story about their discovery and Vinoda's insistence on being brought to the Maṭha so that he might enjoy Bābā's loving service. At the end he said that Vinoda was accustomed to smoke a *hukkā*. As he said this, he brought out the *hukkā* the image used to smoke and some tobacco. But Vinoda was served tobacco in the new *hukkā* brought from Calcutta. The pipe of the *hukkā* was placed in his hand and the door of the altar room closed. After some time, when the door was opened, it was found that the altar-room was filled with smoke and the sweet aroma of tobacco. This happened day after day and many people came to the temple to see the sport of Rādhāvinoda.

One morning Bābā called one of his disciples and said: "Today Śrī Rādhākānta's two other guests will arrive. Make the best possible arrangements for their food. Also keep two garlands ready." He said this and began to move up and down the courtyard eagerly awaiting the arrival of the distinguished guests.

At 9:30 a.m. Haridāsa, a disciple of Bābā, came from Calcutta with two beautiful images of Gaura and Nitāi. He said: "As desired by Gaura and Nitāi I offer myself to you along with them. You do with us whatever you like. I will not go back home."

Gaura and Nitāi were also installed on the altar by the side of Rādhākānta. Now Rādhā and Rādhākānta Deva were the hosts and Rādhā, Rādhāvinoda, Gaura, and Nitāi lived with them as their guests.

Towards the end of his life, when Śrī Rādhāramaṇa Caraṇa Dāsa Deva was living in Navadvīpa, one night Rādhā and Kṛṣṇa appeared to him in a dream and said: "Look, we are in distress. We are lying buried under the floor of the temple of Prāṇakṛṣṇa Mullik in Satgāchiyā. You have to rescue us."

Bābā was overwhelmed. He thought of the miserable condition of the images and wept. Early the next morning he sent a man to Satgāchiyā to call Kuñjadāsa Gosvāmin. When Kuñjadāsa came he asked him to go and bring the images. Kuñjadāsa went with Vipinabihāri Gosvāmin.

Bābā began to wait impatiently for the arrival of the images. He went again and again out of the *āśrama* to see if they were coming. At last he saw Kuñjadāsa and Vipinabihārī Gosvāmins coming with the images. He ran towards them and embraced the images of Rādhā and Rādhākānta. He was enraptured. Physical disturbances (*sāttvika-bhāva*) appeared all over his body.

The images were duly installed after their ritual consecration (*abhiśeka*) in a newly purchased garden, called Rādhāramaṇa Bāga. Adequate arrangements were made for their twenty-four hour service which still continues.

Kṛṣṇa Attracted by Offerings

Kṛṣṇa describes his attraction for offerings lovingly made to him by his devotees in the following words:

> *patraṃ puṣpaṃ phalaṃ toyaṃ*
> *yo me bhaktyā prayacchati*
> *tad ahaṃ bhakty-upahṛtam*
> *aśnāmi prayatātmanaḥ*
>
> Offerings lovingly made to me by my devotee, whatever they may be, fruit, flowers, or even leaves, I accept with pleasure and enjoy.[15]

The proverbial examples of Kṛṣṇa's love for offerings lovingly made are Sudāmā's uncooked rice and the skin of a banana unknowingly offered by Vidura's wife, which Kṛṣṇa ate and enjoyed. Such accounts we read in the *Purāṇas*. We shall here cite some examples from the lives of the devotees who lived in our own times.

---

[15] *Bhagavad-gītā*, 9.26.

Examples

The Khīr of Pisi Mā Gosvāminī

We have already referred to Candraśaśī (Piṣī Mā Gosvāminī) of Delagrāma in the District of Nadiyā and her sacred images Gaura and Nitāi. How the lady, who came from a very respectable family and was heiress to a rich estate, was made by Gaura and Nitāi to renounce the world and go with them to Vṛndāvana so that they might always enjoy her offerings of sweet rice and milk pudding (*khīra*) is a very interesting story.[16]

Candraśaśī once happened to go to Siurī and stay in a house near a temple in which the Gaura and Nitāi images of Murāri Gupta, a companion of Śrī Caitanya Mahāprabhu, were served by Balarāma Dāsa Bābājī, a perfected saint. She saw the beautiful images of Gaura and Nitāi and developed motherly affection for them. She started offering them pudding made every day from forty kilograms of milk.

Once they said to her in a dream: "Mā! We are hungry. We want you to make some pudding to eat." When she told Balarāma Dāsa Bābājī about this he said: "The scriptures forbid the cooking of food for the images by a person not duly initiated." She, therefore, had Balarāma Dāsa Bābājī initiate her and started offering the pudding she had prepared to Gaura and Nitāi. Gaura and Nitāi were now very happy to have a mother who loved them so much. But Candraśaśī was not supposed to stay in Siurī for very long. Gaura and Nitāi knew this. They trembled at the very thought of her going away. One night she saw in a dream both Gaura and Nitāi holding on to the border (*añcala*) of her *sārī* saying: "Mā! Do not go away from here. If you go who will give us pudding every day? Besides, Mā, you are our mother and we are your children. How can children live without their mother?"

Candraśaśī, like a good but helpless mother, caressed them lovingly but pleaded her inability to stay in Siurī indefinitely. She asked them to let go of her *sārī*'s border. But they would not let go. In the tug of war that ensued a piece of her *sārī* was torn off and stayed in Gaura's hands. When Candraśaśī woke up, she saw that a piece of her *sārī* was actually missing. Immediately she went to Balarāma Dāsa Bābājī and told him about it.

---

[16]Haridāsa Dāsa, *Gauḍīya Vaiṣṇava Jīvinī*, vol. 2, 163-170. Kapoor, *The Saints of Vraja*, 127-131.

The day had just dawned. The door of the temple was closed. Balarāma Dāsa Bābā opened the door. Both he and Candraśaśī were surprised to see the torn piece of *sārī* there in Gaura's hand!

Candraśaśī was overwhelmed by a strong current of feeling that in a moment swept away her attachment to home and all its glory and splendor. With determination never to go back she began to live in the temple and serve Gaura and Nitāi with motherly affection. How could she do otherwise after finding children like Gaura and Nitāi?

Candraśaśī was only twenty years old at that time. Her staying alone in the temple with Bābājī aroused suspicion in the minds of people. They began to talk slanderously of her and the Bābā. This pained her very much. One night before going to sleep she wept before Gaura and Nitāi and complained to them of her plight.

The same night Gaura and Nitāi appeared to her in a dream and said, lovingly throwing their arms around her neck: "Mā! Let's go to Vṛndāvana."

So Candraśaśī and Balarāma Dāsa Bābājī took them to Vṛndāvana, where they are now worshiped in a temple in Vanakhaṇḍī. They are known as Piṣī Mā's Gaura and Nitāi because the people of Vṛndāvana called Candraśaśī "Piṣī" Mā (aunty, one's father's sister).

Ṭhākura Madanamohana and the Gūjarī's Milk

During the reign of Haribakṣapāla, the ruler of Karaulī, Madanamohana (Madanagopāla), the image served by Sanātana Gosvāmin was in Karaulī. Śrī Harikiśora Gosvāmin served the image on behalf of the ruler. A *gūjarī*[17] who lived in Bugadār, a village near Karaulī, was a great devotee of Madanamohana. Madanamohana liked her because she was so simple and pure in heart. He often asked her in dream to give him different things to eat. She gladly offered them to him in the temple the next morning. She also gave him some milk every day. She sold milk to a number of persons, but she did not charge for the milk she gave to Madanamohana. On her way to the temple she had to cross a river. She mixed some water from the river with the milk. One day a small fish also got mixed in with the milk without her noticing it. By chance the fish slipped into the milk supplied to Madanamohana. Harikiśora Gosvāmin saw the fish, scolded her, and stopped taking her

[17] A woman belonging to the Gūjara clan of cowherds.

milk.

The Gūjarī felt as if she had been scolded by Madanamohana himself. There was no end to her grief on being deprived of the service of Madanamohana. She gave up food and drink. All day long she lay weeping and praying to the image for forgiveness. She said: "Ṭhākura! I have committed an offense. Forgive me. I have been mixing water with milk every day. You know that I have to do so for my sustenance. I have only one cow and she does not give much milk. If I do not mix water in with it how shall I keep my soul and body together? How shall I do the little service I have been doing for you? You never objected to the milk I supplied. Today unfortunately a fish got into the milk. My only fault was that I did not strain the water. From now on I shall strain the water before mixing it with the milk. But in case you have begun to dislike milk mixed with water, I will not mix it in, even if I have to starve. I shall do as you enjoin. But you must not deprive me of your service. Until you tell me what I should do, I will not eat or drink."

The Gūjarī passed the day like this weeping and sobbing and praying. In the evening she heard someone calling in a sweet voice: "Mā! O Mā!" As she turned her eyes towards the door, she saw a handsome *bābājī* of a tender age looking at her solicitously.

She was compelled to say" "Bābā, come in and sit down."

The *bābā* sat down. The Gūjarī asked: "Bābā, where do you come from? I never saw you before."

"Mā! I live in Vraja. I have come to see Madanamohana. I shall return after the visit tomorrow."

"Mahārāja! Tell me what I can do for you."

"I want a place for the night. I shall be obliged if you kindly let me stay here."

"Bābā, by all means stay. The house is yours."

The *bābā* stayed in the house of the Gūjarī. She asked: "Bābā, what will you eat?"

"Mā, I am a *bābā* who drinks only milk. I do not eat anything else. If you have milk, you can give me some."

"Milk I have, but not fresh milk. After a while I shall feed the cow and milk it. I shall give you fresh milk then."

"Mā! I have not eaten anything since morning. I am very hungry and don't mind stale milk. Come, let me have some."

"Bābā, that milk is not good. I mixed some water in it. There was also a fish in that water."

"So what? You can strain it and give it to me."

"Then, Bābā, let me at least boil the milk. I could not boil it in the morning because my mind was very disturbed."

"Ah! Give me unboiled milk. I am so hungry."

The Gūjarī strained the milk and gave it to the *bābā*. The *bābā* drank and after drinking he looked at the Gūjarī with a smile of deep satisfaction and said: "Mā! Your milk is very tasty."

The *bābā* slept after drinking the milk. The Gūjarī tried to sleep, but could not because of her thirst and hunger. She thought that the *bābā* must be feeling cold because it was winter and she covered him with her worn out quilt.

Towards the end of the night, when she was half-asleep, she saw Madanamohana in a dream. He said: "Gūjarī! Why are you fasting? You think you have been deprived of serving me milk. You were never deprived. You brought milk for me to the temple every day. Yesterday I myself went to your house and drank some. Continue your service. Gosvāmījī will not object. What harm is there if you mix water with the milk? You should just make it more digestible. Now get up and eat some food." With this her sleep was broken. She turned to look at the *bābā*. He was not there. Her quilt was also not there. The *bābā* had left a yellow cloth in place of the quilt. The Gūjarī understood that it was Madanamohana, who came in the guise of the *bābā*. She got up and hurriedly baked two breads. She offered them to Madanamohana and started eating. She was eating and shedding tears of love and joy thinking of Madanamohana's excessive kindness towards her.

In the morning, when Gosvāmījī opened the temple, he was surprised to see Madanamohana wearing a worn out quilt instead of his yellow cloth. This remained a mystery to him until the Gūjarī came with milk and the yellow cloth and said: "Mahārāja! Yesterday Madanamohana came to my house and by mistake left his yellow cloth and took my quilt."

Was it really by mistake that Madanamohana took the Gūjarī's quilt? No. It was as deliberate as his going to her house to drink milk, because he wanted to impress upon the Gosvāmin, who had stopped receiving her milk, that not only her milk but anything she offered was dearer to him than all the precious things offered by him or the king. That was because of her *bhakti*.

Lord Jagannātha and the Khicuri of Karamā Bāi

It is strange that Lord Jagannātha of Purī is offered *khicuri*[18] early in the morning as the first thing to eat. The *khicuri* is called Karamā Bāi's *khicuri*. There is an interesting history behind this practice.[19]

Karamā Bāi was a Jāta[20] widow. She lived in a village called Gadhāmāmoḍa near Alavara. She was poor, but very simple and pure hearted. Her relatives were all dead; yet she lived happily with her sacred image Jagannātha. The world in which she lived was quite different from ours. It was the world of faith, unflinching and unfaltering faith, a world that was governed by love, not by Kali[21] and his agents. Therefore, her ways were different from ours. She did not worship Jagannātha as an image. She regarded him as her beloved child, who depended wholly on her for his care and comfort. She showered all her affection on him. Her devotion to him was natural and spontaneous. So was Jagannātha's love for her. It was bound to be, because he is bound by his own nature to respond to the devotee according to the devotee's feelings and *bhakti*. The feelings of Karamā made him actually behave like her child.

Karamā served him as best she could to make him happy. Jagannātha also did his little bit to serve her and make her happy. Jagannātha was to Karamā the life of her life, the soul of her soul. She did not want him to do anything for her. She even scolded him at times for what he did. But he did not listen. He loved to do all that a child of his tender age could for his mother. He helped her by bringing water in small containers when she was engaged in bathing or feeding her cow. He helped her by picking up twigs in the forest when she went there to collect firewood. He helped her in whatever way he could when she cooked food or washed utensils or did anything else.

But he pestered her much early in the morning when he got hungry. He was very fond of *khicuri*. He made her get up from bed early and prepare *khicuri*, without bathing, without changing her clothes and without cleaning the kitchen first as Indian ladies are required to do, specially when they are to cook for the sacred images. He kept on pestering her

---

[18] A boiled mixture the consistency of pudding made from rice, lentils, and salt.

[19] *Bhakta-māla*, 50; Kapoor, *Navabhaktamāla.*, 196-7.

[20] A caste or birth-community of people in India.

[21] A personification of the Age of Kali, the age of "ones" or the losing die in the game of dice. If one rolls a "one," that is, if the side of the die that only has one dot on it comes up, one loses in the Indian game of dice. Thus, the Age of Kali is the unlucky or losing age. We are said to be living in the Age of Kali now, according to Hindu chronology. [Ed.]

until *khicuri* was prepared and offered to him.

Once Karamā went to Purī to witness the Rathayātrā (Festival of Chariots) of Lord Jagannātha of Purī along with her own Jagannātha. When she was looking at the big image of Lord Jagannātha in the temple, the thought came to her mind that perhaps that Jagannātha was different from her own Jagannātha. Immediately she saw her own Jagannātha seated in the place of Lord Jagannātha and her doubt disappeared.

We do not know whether it was because Lord Jagannātha wanted to strengthen Karamā's belief in his identity with her own Jagannātha or because he could not resist the temptation of her *khicuri*, but he began to go to her every morning to eat the *khicuri* she offered to her own Jagannātha. The time suited him well because he could go in the morning to eat and return before the time of *rāja-bhoga*[22] in the temple.

One day a holy man happened to visit Karamā. He saw that Karamā prepared *khicuri* without bathing and without cleaning the kitchen and offered the food to Jagannātha. He rebuked her for her sins and told her that she had been committing an offense by not following the rituals as laid down in the scriptures, for which she would have to go to hell. Karamā was frightened. She learned the rituals from the holy man. The next day she followed the ritualistic procedure. Therefore, the offering was greatly delayed. Lord Jagannātha had begun to like Karamā's *khicuri* so much that it had become a habit with him to go to her at the usual time and return after eating the food offered by her. That day also he came at the usual time, but had to return to the temple, because he saw that Karamā was bathing. He came again after some time, but had to return because he saw that she was cleaning the kitchen. In this way he had to come and go back several times until at last he found the offering ready. He fell upon it as soon as it was offered. He had eaten only a little while when the *rāja-bhoga* bell rang in the temple. He had to go back at once, because the *pūjārī* (ritual worshiper) who offered the main offering (*rāja-bhoga*) was also as good a devotee as Karamā and he had to reach the temple in time to enjoy the food lovingly offered by him and to avoid his displeasure. In haste he forgot to wash his mouth.[23] When the *pūjārī* was about to offer the food he was surprised to see that Jagannātha's mouth was stained with *khicuri*. He said to him: "Prabhu!

[22]The big daily offerings of food in the Jagannātha temple. It literally means the king's meal.

[23]*Rāmarasikāvalī*, 630; *Nava-bhakta-mālā*, 198.

Why is your mouth stained with *khicuri*? Have you gone somewhere else to eat? Do you not like the offerings I make for you?" The Lord like one who has a guilty conscience kept quiet. But the *pūjārī* had to have an answer. He closed the door of the altar room without offering the *rāja-bhoga* and went and sat outside determined not to offer food until Lord Jagannātha revealed his secret. Jagannātha had eaten only a few morsels of *khicuri*. Therefore he was hungry. How long could he remain hungry? How long could he keep thousands of his devotees hungry, who ate his *prasāda* (grace-food, remnants of food offered to the sacred image) every day? How could he displease the *pūjārī*, whom he loved as much as he loved Karamā?

He broke his silence. The *pūjārī* heard him say: "Pūjārījī! Come, offer the food. I am hungry. I acknowledge my guilt. Every morning I go to eat Karamā's *khicuri* and return in time for the main offering. I returned late today. But the fault is not mine. Every day Karamā prepared *khicuri* without bathing and without observing all the rules and regulations of ritualistic service. Today the offering was delayed because she followed the rituals under the advice of a holy man. The holy man does not know that I relish even the ordinary fare offered by love more than the richest food offered ceremoniously according to the rituals. The rituals prescribed by the scriptures are essential, but only as long as the seed of love has not sprouted in the heart. Rituals have no place in love. Both my devotee and I dance as love makes us dance. I smell the scent of Karamā's *khicuri* offered lovingly to me from here and cannot resist the temptation of enjoying the offering. Her *khicuri* attracts me even as a magnet attracts iron and I am mechanically drawn towards it. I do not go of my own accord. You go and tell that holy man that he should ask Karamā to prepare the *khicuri* offering as she was doing it before. Rituals are important, but not for her."

Karamā remained in Purī and Lord Jagannātha enjoyed her *khicuri* offerings every day. One day she left her body. Jagannātha fasted that day.[24]

It had become Jagannātha's habit to eat Karamā's *khicuri*. He could not remain without it. One may get over any other habit, but the habit formed by love cannot be gotten over. One day Jagannātha told the ritual servants of the temple: "it is not possible for me to live without eating Karamā's *khicuri*. You must offer me *khicuri* every day in her

---

[24] *Rāmarasikāvalī*, 631.

name at the very time she used to offer it." Since then Jagannātha is offered *khicuri* early in the morning as the first thing to eat.

Govindadeva and the Gardener's Pomegranate

During the reign of Aurangzeb Rūpa Gosvāmin's sacred image, Śrī Govinda Deva, was taken to Jaipur. Mahārāja Jai Sinha of Jaipur built a new temple for him and appointed Śrī Govindacaraṇa Gosvāmin as the *pūjārī* in charge of his service.

One morning when Gosvāmījī opened the door of the altar-room for the morning service (*maṅgala-ārati*), he was surprised to see that the clothes of Govinda Deva were torn. How strange! The clothes were not torn when he put him to bed the previous night. It could not be the work of a mouse, because the cut was in a long, straight line. It looked as if Govindajī had gone out somewhere and tore his clothes because they had become entangled with something. Could Govindajī get out when the door was closed and locked from the outside? No one else could have torn the clothes, because no one was in the altar-room after the door was closed.

Gosvāmījī did not take long to solve the mystery. He was not an ordinary *pūjārī*, but an accomplished (*siddha*) saint.[25] He went into trance (*samādhi*). In trance Rādhā said to him: "Last night we both went to a garden to pick pomegranates. Lālajī (Kṛṣṇa) had picked only one when the gardener came to know of it. He ran after us with his stick. We fled. Though the pomegranate was green, Lālajī still ate it." Gosvāmījī then looked all around the throne of the sacred image. He was surprised to see the rind of the pomegranate and its seeds scattered all over.

Immediately Gosvāmījī called the gardener. He asked him: "Did anyone go to your garden yesterday to pick pomegranates?"

"Yes, Mahārāja! A boy and a girl went there. When I ran towards them with my stick, they fled."

"Oh! How fortunate you are, gardener. Yet, how unfortunate! The Lord and his beloved themselves went to your garden and you chased them away with your stick."

"What? What, Mahārāja? The Lord and his beloved?"

[25] See *Nava-bhakta-māla*, Part II, 298-305.

"Yes, yes, the Lord and his beloved. Come and see what is lying here — the seeds of an unripe pomegranate. They brought it here and ate it."

The gardener was a great devotee of Govindajī. He went to the temple to see Govindajī whenever there was a service (*ārati*), unmindful of sun, rain or storm.

Rūpa Gosvāmin has issued a warning regarding the seeing of Govindajī in his famous *smerāṃ bhaṅgī-traya-paricitām* verse.[26] He said: "My friend! If you want to live happily with your wife and children, relations and friends, do not look at the image called Govinda, who stands at Keśī Tīrtha in the threefold bending posture, with peacock feather on his head and a flute at his lips, looking sideways at you with a mischievous smile. If once you look at him you will forget all your kith and kin and the joy of life." This is what happens to a person who looks at Govindajī but once. But the gardener used to see him every day a number of times. He was bound to forget his wife and children and everything else and think all the time of Govinda, live all the time for Govinda and do all that he could for Govinda and Govinda alone.

He had planted for Govinda several pomegranate trees in his garden. He was anxiously waiting for the day when the trees would grow and bear fruit and he would offer them to Govinda. His anxiety to make the offering of pomegranates to Govinda was bound to produce anxiety to receive and enjoy the offering of love in the mind of Govinda, for such is the law of reciprocation of *bhakti*, of which we shall speak in detail later. Govinda's anxiety was ten times stronger than the gardener's. He was closely watching the growth of the trees. His heart sprang with joy when he saw flowers on the trees. The flowers gradually turned into fruit. The fruit would take some time to ripen. But Govinda did not have the patience to wait until then. He went to the garden, picked a green pomegranate and ate it.

When Gosvāmījī told the gardener about this sport of Govinda and the gardener saw the seeds of the unripe pomegranate lying near the throne of Govinda, he was overwhelmed with emotion. Tears began to stream from his eyes. His hairs stood on end. He kept looking at Govinda. He wanted to say something, but he could not. He managed to say: "Govinda, Govinda!" and fell unconscious on the ground. On regaining consciousness, he said: "Ṭhākura! You came, but I did not

---

[26]Rūpa Gosvāmin, *Bhakti-rasāmṛta-sindhu*, 1.2.239.

recognize you. I should have spread my heart on the ground to welcome you, but I ran after you with my stick. I thought you were the children of some maid-servant of the palace and began to shower abuses on you. The trees and the pomegranates are yours. They were planted for you. But you came like a thief, perhaps because you did not want me to recognize you. What did you gain by concealing yourself from me and from hearing all my abuses?"

The gardener did not know that Govinda enjoys the abuses of a devotee even more than his praises. He did not know that he enjoys stealing what belongs to a devotee more than begging for it. When did he beg for the butter of the cowherd women of Vraja? He always stole it. He was, therefore, called the butter-thief (*makhana-cora*). A thief feels offended if you call him a thief. But this thief is different from the others. He feels happy when you call him a thief.

When Mahārāja Jai Sinha learned about the theft, he gave the gardener a piece of land in reward, because he had grown trees the fruit of which Govinda could not help stealing. His descendents are even now enjoying the yield of the land.

Kṛṣṇa Attracted by Dance, *Kīrtana* and Talks

Kṛṣṇa's attraction for the dance and *kīrtana* (glorification in song) of his devotees and for their talks and discourses about him and his sports is unique. He describes it thus:

> *nāhaṃ vasāmi vaikuṇṭhe yogināṃ hṛdaye na ca*
> *mad-bhaktā yatra gāyanti tatra tiṣṭhāmi nārada*
>
> I live neither in Vaikuṇṭha nor in the heart of the yogīs. I go and sit where my devotees are singing, Nārada.[27]
>
> *gītvā ca mama nāmāni nartyen mama sannidhau*
> *idaṃ bravīmi te satyaṃ krīto 'haṃ tena cārjuna*
>
> Listen Arjuna! I tell you truthfully that one who sings my names and dances before me purchases me.[28]

[27] *Padma Purāṇa* cited in the *Bhakti-sandarbha*, verse 827.
[28] *ādi Purāṇa* cited in the *Hari-bhakti-vilāsa* at 11.446.

> *gītvā ca mama nāmāni rudanti mama sannidhau*
> *teṣām ahaṃ parikrīto nānya-krīto janārdanaḥ*
>
> And one who sings my names and cries before me completely purchases me, though I am Janārdana, and I am sold to no one else.[29]
>
> *śṛṇvataḥ śraddhayā nityaṃ gṛṇataś ca sva-ceṣṭitam*
> *nātidīrgheṇa kālena bhagavān viśate hṛdi*
>
> The Lord soon enters the heart of one who always listens to and narrates his acts.[30]

Following are some examples of the law of gravitation in this form.

Examples

The Song of the Cowherd Girls and Śrī Kṛṣṇa

One of the finest examples of the influence the song of the devotee exercises on Kṛṣṇa is the *Gopī-gīta* (the Song of the Cowherd Girls) on the full moon night on which the Circle Dance (*rāsa-līlā*) took place. That night, while Kṛṣṇa was engaged in different kinds of amorous sports with them, he suddenly disappeared. The cowherd girls went around the forest in search of him, weeping and moaning and making enquiries from the animals, the trees and the vines, as if they had gone mad. They did not find him anywhere. Greatly struck with grief and disappointment they sat down on the bank of the Yamunā. In their moment of intense suffering they thought that the only thing that could relieve their pain and prevent life from running out of them was a song about Kṛṣṇa. So they began to sing in sweet and sonorous voices a song relating to the sports of Kṛṣṇa. The song touched the tender-most corner of Kṛṣṇa's heart and created such an upheaval in it that he could no longer remain in hiding. He appeared before them. With his appearance the cowherd girls felt that life, which had almost left them, had returned. One of the cowherd girls quickly spread her upper cloth on the ground for him to sit on and he sat down with a captivating smile on his lips.

---

[29] *ādi Purāṇa* cited in the *Hari-bhakti-vilāsa* at 11.447.
[30] Bhāg., 2.8.3.

"How surprising," it is said in the *Bhāgavata*, "that Bhagavān Kṛṣṇa, who does not condescend to sit even on the altars of the hearts of the greatest yogīs, purified by life-long practice, readily sat on the cloth of the cowherd girl stained with the powder of her body, completely charmed and enslaved by the song of the cowherd girls."[31]

Stories about Kṛṣṇa

One night Kṛṣṇa was asleep in his royal seraglio in Dvārakā,[32] when the queens heard him sigh and cry out: "Where are you, my beloved? Where are you, Rādhā?" Rukmiṇī[33] touched his feet and roused him.

The queens asked him why he was crying and for whom. Kṛṣṇa felt ashamed. He simply said he did not know and went to sleep again. The queens were not satisfied with his evasive answer. They talked among themselves. One of them said: "Who might this fortunate lady be, who has captured the heart of our lord? She must be extraordinarily fair and accomplished. But we are all princesses. Royal blood runs in our veins. We are in no way inferior to anyone. How does it happen then that our lord is hopelessly in love with another lady? He thinks of her by day and dreams of her by night. Who is this lady who casts us into shadow and wins his heart?"

Rukmiṇī said: "I have heard of Rādhā, a cowherd girl of Vṛndāvana, with whom our lord was in love when he was there. He may be thinking of her. Perhaps he has not been able to forget her even in our company."

Satyabhāmā[34] said: "But she is after all only a cowherd girl. Is it possible that our lord should prefer a shepardess to the galaxy of princesses in his own harem? Let us do one thing. Mother Rohiṇī is here with us and she was there in Vṛndāvana. She knows it all. Let us go to her."

The next afternoon, when Kṛṣṇa was holding court, his queens went to mother Rohiṇī, told her what had happened, and begged her to relate Kṛṣṇa's love sports of Vṛndāvana. She agreed, but she enjoined them to be strictly on guard against the approach of Śrī Kṛṣṇa and Balarāma, who would be inevitably drawn by the power of the love-tale to hear

[31]ibid., 10.32.14.

[32]Dvārakā is a place in modern Gujarat where Kṛṣṇa the king is said to have moved his capital from Mathurā.

[33]The chief of the queens of Kṛṣṇa.

[34]The most beloved and spirited queen of Kṛṣṇa.

it. She could not as their mother tell the tale of their love-making before her sons. Accordingly Subhadrā, the sister of Kṛṣṇa and Balarāma, was stationed as a sentinel at the door with strict orders not to let her brothers in under any pretext as long as the tale was being told.

The mother sat in the center and the queens in a circle around her. She then proceeded to unfold the amorous tale. The charm of the tale was irresistible. Kṛṣṇa and Balarāma left the court and ran to the spot where they found Subhadrā guarding the door. They asked her to stand aside and let them pass. But she said that mother Rohiṇī had bidden them not to enter at that time. They were not expected to know the reason, but they must obey. So they obeyed. But they could not but remain standing there listening to the delectable conversation between their mother and the queens.

When their mother started describing the *rāsa-līlā* (Circle Dance), all the signs and symptoms of love (the *sāttvika-bhāvas*) became manifest in the bodies of Kṛṣṇa and Balarāma. Streams of tears began to flow from their eyes. The sight of that brought tears to Subhadrā's eyes as well. All three started shedding tears — copious tears of love and joy. When Rohiṇī began to explain the utter self-forgetfulness of Rādhā's love, Balarāma could no longer contain himself. He was lost and convulsed with indrawn passion. His limbs were drawn into his body on account of the current of internal commotion that raged in his heart. Śrī Kṛṣṇa was affected in a similar manner. His hands and feet were also shrunken and indrawn. Subhadrā was spell-bound and rooted to the spot where she stood. Sudarśana[35] itself was melted and lengthened.[36]

Then came Nārada[37] to visit with the Lord of Dvārakā. He went to the court. There they told him that the Lord was in his palace. He had the privilege of entering the harem. So he entered. Coming to the doorway he saw the sight and stood stock still, for he had never seen anything like what met his eyes at that time. When Rohiṇī changed the theme and spoke of Rādhā's distress after her separation from Kṛṣṇa, all four came back to themselves and regained their former condition.

---

[35]This is the name of the discus of Kṛṣṇa, his characteristic weapon.

[36]We know it as a historical fact, recorded by eye-witnesses, that Śrī Caitanya also was sometimes found in this condition — "like a tortoise in its shell."

[37]The devotee sage (*ṛṣi*), one of the primordial sages, born from the thought of Brahmā, the creator of the world. He carries the *vīṇā* (a stringed instrument) in his hands, which he plays as he sings hymns in praise of the Lord. He wanders wherever he wishes to in the entire system of the fourteen planes of existence to help the manifestation of the sports of the Lord.

Nārada at that time began to sing songs in praise of the Lord. The Lord was pleased. He said: "Nārada! You have come at this golden moment. You can ask for any boon you want." Nārada asked him to explain what he had seen. Kṛṣṇa explained how what he saw was due to the influence of the narration by mother Rohiṇī of his love-sport, which had melted his form and changed it. Nārada then asked for the boon that the quadruple forms, melted in love, which he had seen might be manifested on Earth in wood so that all might see them. The boon was granted. The manifestation of Kṛṣṇa in the form that we see in Lord Jagannātha in Purī reminds us of the spell that stories of his own playful activities place him under.[38]

Recitation of the *Bhāgavata*

Śrī Avadha Dāsa Bābā was a perfected saint who lived in Dhobi Gali in Vṛndāvana until 1937, when he passed away at the age of 110.[39] His worship consisted exclusively of recitation and worship of the *Bhāgavata Purāṇa*. He worshiped the *Bhāgavata* in exactly the same manner in which the sacred image of Śrī Kṛṣṇa is worshiped, because he regarded the *Bhāgavata* as a manifestation of Śrī Kṛṣṇa himself. He wrapped it in a silken cloth, placed it on a decorated altar, offered food to it and ate its remnants as "grace-food" (*prasāda*). He fanned it in summer, covered it with a quilt in the winter and swung it on a swing in the rainy season.

He did not spend a single minute without doing ritual worship (*pūjā*) or recitation of the *Bhāgavata*. He recited the verses of the *Bhāgavata* and turned the pages without looking at them, for he not only knew all the verses by heart, he knew also the verses with which each page began and ended. While reciting the *Bhāgavata* he meditated on the sport of Kṛṣṇa and imagined that he was reciting it to Kṛṣṇa. Meditation was not for him simply a mental exercise. He actually saw the sport and participated in it.

This is clear from a particular episode. Once a young man came to his hermitage (*āśrama*). He had heard that if one ate the remains of food eaten by a perfected saint he would be blessed with a vision of Kṛṣṇa. He came at the time when Bābā was eating grace-food. He went straight to him, though he was asked by Bābā's disciple not to go near him while

---

[38] *Carita-sudhā*, 49-51.

[39] Kapoor, *Vraja ke Bhakt*, vol. 1, 366-73.

he was eating. He sat before him and with folded hands requested a little grace-food out of his plate. But Bābā was lost in divine sport even while he was eating. The young man thought that Bābā had ignored his request. He stretched out his hand and took some grace-food from the plate. As he was about to eat the grace-food, Bābā caught his hand. But he opened his fist and quickly taking the grace-food in the other hand put it in his mouth and swallowed it down.

As soon as he put the grace-food in his mouth he became unconscious. He remained unconscious until late in the evening. When Bābā had finished his evening reading of the *Bhāgavata*, he asked the holy men (*sādhu*) who had come as usual to attend the reading to perform sacred singing (*kīrtana*) around him. As the singing began the young man opened his eyes. For some time he looked all around in bewilderment. Then suddenly taking hold of Bābā's feet he wept and said: "Pardon me Mahārāja. I have committed a great offense at your feet. But now I have come to know about your real nature. I shall remain at your feet and serve you all my life. I shall not go anywhere else. You will have to accept me. Have mercy, *gurudeva*; have mercy on me!."

Bābā not only pardoned him, he gave him initiation and took the entire responsibility for his spiritual welfare upon himself. One of the holy men asked the young man what he had come to know about Bābā. "As soon as I put the remains of Bābā's food in my mouth, I was transported to an otherworldly region. There I saw that Śrī Kṛṣṇa's midday sport of eating was going on in a forest. Bābā and Kṛṣṇa were sitting in the middle, surrounded by friends and in an atmosphere of joviality and mirth, both were putting the remains of their food into each other's mouths with their hands."

Śrī Kṛṣṇa came every day to listen to the reading of the *Bhāgavata* by Avadha Dāsa Bābā and sat somewhere unnoticed by the other listeners. Perhaps Bābā alone could see him. One day he saw Śrī Kṛṣṇa circumambulating the *Bhāgavata* after the reading was over. It was strange and striking, because it is always the worshiper who circumambulates the object he worships. Did Śrī Kṛṣṇa regard the *Bhāgavata* as an object of his worship?

The answer is obvious. The *Bhāgavata* is not only a manifestation of Kṛṣṇa in words. It is also a manifestation in words of divine love (*preman*). Divine love is the end, not only for finite selves, but also for Kṛṣṇa. The *Bhāgavata* depicts Kṛṣṇa's love-sports with his devotees. Therefore, he regards his own manifestation as the *Bhāgavata* as superior to himself. Therefore also, he is always eager to listen to the recitation of the *Bhāgavata*. The recitation of the *Bhāgavata* by his perfected devotees has an additional attraction for him. Śrī Jīva Gosvāmin depicts him in the *Gopāla-campū* as listening with great zest to the stories of his love-sports with his devotees from Madhukaṇṭha and Snigdhakaṇṭha even in Goloka.

The *Saṅkīrtana* of Ṭhākura Candra Sinha

Ṭhākura Candra Sinha, born in 1888, was the chief of Kaḍvārī, a state under Mahārāja Gaṅgā Sinha, the ruler of Bikāner. He was held in high esteem by the Mahārāja and was appointed Home Secretary by him. Later he became a member of the Legislative Council. He was known as an able administrator and a good social worker. But no one knew that he concealed behind his outward appearance the heart of a devotee. The devotee in him could not remain concealed for long. In 1919, when his brother died, it appeared with a burst. He stopped all external activities, took initiation from Śrī Śyāma Dāsa, a famous saint of the Śuka Sampradāya (community) and applied himself exclusively to worship. He did not waste a single minute without engaging in worship. His day began with singing the Lord's names and sports (*saṅkīrtana*), which continued from 3:30 to 7:00 a.m. The singing was open to all, but only six or seven devotees attended it regularly.

One day in the winter season it rained torrentially from 2:00 to 7:00 a.m. It was impossible for the devotees to leave their homes. Candra Sinhajī sang alone for some time, expecting that the rain would slacken and at least one or two persons would come. But the rain did not let up. Sometime later, however, the drum player came with an umbrella, somewhat drenched and shivering. He said, "Excuse me Ṭhākura Sāhib. I am late. I was waiting for the rain to stop or let up. But it didn't. I have somehow managed to come." Ṭhākura Sāhib said: "I am happy that you have come, but you must be wet to the skin."

"No, not much" replied the drummer and sat down after offering obeisance before the picture of Śrī Kṛṣṇa. The singing began. That day the drummer's performance was superb. He seemed to be inspired. He would at times fill with inspiration and look at Ṭhākura Sāhib. Ṭākura Sāhib would also become inspired and look at him. Each inspired the other. Although there were only two instruments that day, the drum and the harmonium which Ṭhākura Sāhib played, that day's enjoyment in singing surpassed the enjoyment of all the other days.

The drummer departed at the conclusion of the singing, but left Ṭhākura Sāhib in a half-conscious state, still enjoying the sounds of the singing.

The next morning, when the regular members of the singing group assembled, they expressed regret for not being able to come on the previous day. The drummer also said: "Ṭhākura Sāhib. I am sorry I also was not able to come, because it was raining so heavily."

Ṭhākura Sāhib said with a start: "What? Are you in your senses? Did you not come yesterday?"

"You must have seen me in a dream, Ṭhākura Sāhib. It is no surprise that your fondness for singing the Lord's names makes you enjoy it even in your sleep."

Ṭhākura Sāhib began to think: "Is it true that I saw a dream?" But the next moment he burst out: "No, no, not a dream. You actually came and played the drum such as you have never played before. I never enjoyed singing as much as I did yesterday."

The mystery of the drummer deepened. As everyone was looking at Ṭhākura Sāhib and the drummer with bewilderment, a current passed through the veins of every member of the group. The drummer was inspired to speak aloud and say: "It was no other than Kṛṣṇa himself who came as the drummer. It is no wonder that he came and accompanied a lover of the singing of the Lord's names like Ṭhākura Sāhib. Has he not said: *mad-bhaktā yatra gāyanti tatra tiṣṭhāmi nārada* — I go and sit wherever my devotees sing. He must already have been here to listen to the singing. When no one turned up to accompany Ṭhākura Sāhib, how could he restrain himself from appearing in person in the guise of the drummer and playing the drum? Let us say: 'Victory to Śrī Kṛṣṇacandra!'" Everyone cried aloud: "Victory to Śrī Kṛṣṇacandra!"

The *Saṅkīrtana* of Harisevakajī

Harisevakajī was a simple-hearted devotee who lived in Thānā, a village in the state of Alavar. He once heard a song of the saint Śrī Caraṇa Dāsajī which created a sweet disturbance in his heart. The burden of the song was:

> Blessed is the devotee who desires nothing
> But sings always the praises of the Lord.

For him the Lord blesses soon
And embraces close to his heart.

"Does the Lord really embrace the man who wants nothing and sings his praises?" he went and asked Caraṇa Dāsajī.

Caraṇa Dāsajī replied: "Indeed! The Lord is so pleased with the person who wants nothing except him and sings his names and praises that he comes and embraces him."

"But I see some people passionately singing his praises and shedding tears as they sing, yet the Lord neither comes nor embraces them."

"That is because their hearts are not pure. They are filled with desires other than the attainment of the lotus feet of the Lord. Singing in praise (*kīrtana*) gradually purifies the heart. When the heart is purified the Lord comes. He cannot but come and embrace one. Singing in praise is the easiest way to attain him. It is easier to attain him through singing than to attain any other end through any other means, because when you pursue some other end it is you who moves towards the end. The end does not move towards you. But when you sing with earnest desire to find the Lord, the Lord also becomes anxious to find you. He moves even faster towards you than you move towards him."

Harisevakajī took his words to heart. He took initiation from Caraṇa Dāsajī and started going from village to village dancing and singing. Wherever he went he sang in praise and asked people to participate. He told them that in singing about Hari Śrī Kṛṣṇa was always present. But people did not believe him. He prayed to the Lord to give him proof of his presence. Once when he was thus praying in his heart and singing and dancing in praise, the Lord came and embraced him and disappeared. Before disappearing he threw his yellow cloth over Harisevakajī. No one could see Kṛṣṇa except Harisevakajī. But everyone saw the yellow cloth. Everyone was then convinced of Kṛṣṇa's presence in the singing of His praise.

The yellow cloth remained with Harisevakajī until the end but disappeared with him when he breathed his last.

Verification of the Law of Reciprocation

According to the law of reciprocation, Bhagavān reciprocates the attitude of the *bhakta* as well as the non-*bhakta* and the non-believers. For those who do not believe in his existence he is non-existent. He ignores them just as they ignore him. He leaves them to their fate and they suffer pain and pleasure, birth and death until the strokes of *māyā* bring them to their senses and they not only recognize Bhagavān but surrender to him.

For those who believe in the existence of Bhagavān, but do not believe in the sacred image, which is for them but a piece of stone, the image is stone. But for those who regard even a piece of stone as Bhagavān, the stone is not stone but Bhagavān. This is evident from the life of Dhannā Jāta, a famous disciple of ācārya Rāmānanda of the Śrī Sampradāya. We shall begin with Dhannā in citing examples of Bhagavān's reciprocation in love.

Examples

Ṭhākura and Dhannā Jāta

Dhannā was the son of Pannā Jāta and his wife Rekhā who lived in Dhuvana, a village in the district of Tonka of Rajasthan. He was only four or five years old when one day, his family guru came to his house. The guru had his sacred image, a Śālagrāma stone, with him. While the guru was worshiping the stone, Dhannā sat near him and watched. After he had completed his worship, Dhannā said: "Now I shall worship." The guru said: "No. Children do not worship." But Dhannā would not listen. The guru said: "Alright. Wait a little while. I shall give you another image." He went out and brought from somewhere a black stone. He put the stone on a improvised altar and the Śālagrāma stone down below in front of the altar and said: "Look here Dhannā. This image on the altar is Rājā Ṭhākura and the one below is Sipāhī (constable) Ṭhākura. Which image will you take?" Now Dhannā knew the difference between the Rājā (king) and the Sipāhī (constable). He said: " I will take the Rājā Ṭhākura."

Dhannā was happy. He went to his mother and said: " Mā! Gurujī has given me Rājā Ṭhākura. Give me materials for his worship." The mother laughed it away, but Dhannā persisted in his demand. Only to get rid of him his mother said: "I shall get them from the market tomorrow morning. The market is closed today."

That night Dhannā cried out several times in his sleep: "Mā, it is now morning. Get me the materials from the market." When day actually dawned it was difficult for his mother to contain him. She said in desperation: "Ṭhākura is not pleased with the materials supplied by others. The worshiper has to collect the materials himself."

Dhannā started his search for the materials. There were some flower plants outside his home. He collected flowers from them. He could not distinguish between *tulasī* (sacred basil) leaves and other leaves. He collected any leaves that he could get. For incense sticks also he collected any sticks that he could find. As for the sandal paste he consoled himself with the thought that the sacred image liked red paste more than white. He made some red paste from bricks and water. He bathed his image in water, then offered him flowers and applied the red sandal paste on his forehead. Yes, it was red sandal paste for him. And for the image? How was the image concerned with it all? Was not the so-called image only a stone from the street which must have been kicked by men and animals times beyond number? No. The supreme being had manifested himself in the stone the moment Dhannā hugged it lovingly as his lord. How could he restrain himself from reciprocating the love and faith of the innocent, artless, and guileless Dhannā? And if the brick paste was sandal paste for Dhannā, how could it be otherwise for the image?

After the worship was over, Dhannā offered his image a food-offering of Bejhara breads and molasses given to him by his mother and drew the curtains before the image. After some time he peeped in to see whether the image was eating or not. Seeing that he was not eating, he begged him again and again to eat. The image did not, because he relished the impatience and restlessness of the *bhakta* and tried to augment it as much as possible. But how could Dhannā continue to entreat him? In desperation he said: "Don't eat then. I will also not eat." He lay down on the ground with his back against the image, weeping and sobbing.

The sacred image could not tolerate this. He started eating. He ate the bread with such an action of the jaws that it produced a munching sound, which Dhannā could hear. With a start he sat up and lifted the curtain a little. What met his eyes this time was something he had never imagined. He saw the image munching on the bread and smilingly looking at him. He said: "Dhannā! Your bread is very sweet." Tears of love and joy trickled down from the eyes of Dhannā. He was dazed and enthralled by the resplendent beauty of the image's smiling face and the exceedingly sweet tone of his voice. He kept on looking at the image for some time and the image kept on looking at him. Both looked at each other with love. They felt they were sold to each other because of each other's love.

Dhannā offered food to his image every day and every day he saw him eating and admiring the simple fare Dhannā offered him to eat. As the days rolled on the bond of love between them strengthened to the extent that they became bosom friends.

Dhannā had not practiced any spiritual discipline. His heart was pure and he had unflinching faith in the words of the guru. The sacred image was sold out to the spontaneous outflow of devotion from his heart, free from the observance of the rules and regulations of ritualistic *bhakti*. Dhannā did not know who the image really was. He did not know the meaning of the words "sacred image" (*ṭhākura*) or "God" (*bhagavān*). These were to him the different names by which his friend was called. So the sacred image was to him his friend and that was all.

Their friendship became more and more intimate. The image became the constant companion and playmate of Dhannā. When Dhannā grew a little older the image started going with him to the pasture for pasturing the cows of his father.

Slowly Dhannā came to know that Bhagavān and Ṭhākura meant the great Lord, who was the creator and destroyer of the universe and that his friend was no other than the Lord himself. The knowledge brought about a change in the feeling of Dhannā. His friendship with the image began to shrink. He could not remain as free in his behavior towards him as he used to be. A corresponding change in the image's feeling towards him was inevitable. He was no more his constant companion. He only appeared occasionally for a short while and disappeared. This made Dhannā very unhappy.

This would not have happened if the knowledge that came to Dhannā was true knowledge. It was not knowledge but ignorance. Bhagavān in his true self is not the creator and destroyer. Creation and destruction are functions of his partial manifestations. In his true self he is *rasa* (rapture) and *rasika*, the supreme enjoyer of *rasa*. He does not realize his nature as *rasa* in creation and destruction but in the loving relationship with his *bhaktas*. When does Bhagavān, who is simply Bhagavān but not a friend, eat or play with anyone?

There was no end to Dhannā's suffering in separation from his sacred image. To mitigate his suffering he began to cultivate the company of the saintly (*sādhus*). Still, the suffering became more and more intense. In the end he lost his desire for sleep and food. It became difficult for him to keep body and soul together.

Then the image appeared to him in a dream one day and said: "Dhannā, I am not displeased with you. But you lack one thing, on account of which I cannot always be as free with you as I was before. The kind of permanent relationship you want to establish with me is not possible without the guru. You go to Kāśī and take initiation from Śrī Rāmānandācārya. Then your desire shall be fulfilled."

So Dhannā went to Kāśī and took initiation from Rāmānandācārya. When he returned, his Lord in his image appeared before him, embraced him and became his constant companion as before. Dhannā's attitude towards him, which had become conditioned and constrained on account of knowledge of his godliness, became, by the grace of his guru, as spontaneous and natural as before. But the image was somewhat unhappy because Dhannā now served him but avoided being served. So the image sometimes fulfilled his desire to serve him disguised as someone else.

Once Dhannā's father gave him some seeds to plant in a field. As he was about to plant the seeds in the field some saints came to him and said: "We are going to your house because we are hungry and want something to eat." Dhannā boiled the seeds and fed them. After a couple of months he was surprised to see a good crop coming up in the field, even though he had not sown a single seed. He thought that it must be due to the blessings of the saints whom he had fed with the seeds. He planted the seeds in the mouths of the saints, but they grew in the fields.

Dhannā began to look for a man to guard the field and protect it from animals. A man came and said: "Dhannājī, I understand that you want a watchman for your field. I am a good watchman. I can offer my services, if you promise to give me a share of the crop."

"What share do you want?"

"One-third of the crop."

"That is too much. I can give you one-fourth."

"No, Dhannājī, you know how strenuous the job is. One has to be awake and alert throughout the day and night."

"Very well. I shall give you one-third but nothing besides."

"Yes. Nothing besides, but you must give me my meals morning and evening."

"You mean I must serve you as much as you serve me?"

"You see, I do not have a wife to cook and bring me my meals. If I go home and cook them myself both times, who will watch the field?"

"Alright. I shall bring you bread both times. Nothing else I hope."

"And breakfast, too: only two pieces of bread and butter."

"Breakfast, too?"

"You see, that way I shall see a saint like you early in the morning and shall be more energized for work. In fact, it is the attraction of seeing you several times during the day that makes me want to work for you. Otherwise, you know, there are many others who want me to work for them."

"Very well, Bābā. I shall bring you your breakfast also. Start work today. What is your name?"

"Saunjhiyā."

Saunjhiyā began to work as Dhannā's watchman in the field. Dhannā brought him his breakfast and meals regularly. One day, when harvesting time was near, he brought breakfast earlier than usual, because he had to cook for some saints whom he had invited for dinner. At that time Saunjhiyā was asleep. He had covered himself with his quilt. Dhannā said: "Get up, Saunjhiyā, and have your breakfast."

As he said this he pulled the quilt back. He was aghast to see that it was his sacred image, not Saunjhiyā. "Lord! You!"

The image immediately turned into Saunjhiyā and said: "Excuse me, Bhagatjī, for default in service. I was awake the whole night and therefore slept for a short while."

"No more, Lord. You cannot deceive me any more. You will no longer guard my field."

"What?! Now, when the crop is to be harvested and I have to get my share of the produce, you will dismiss me? I will not let you cheat me like that. I shall invoke the village council."

"Who has cheated, Lord, you or I? Which village council shall I invoke for having been cheated by you? You must now give up this guise of Saunjhiyā, the cheat, and reappear as my sacred image. I shall not eat or drink until you do. I shall starve myself to death if you do not appear as my image." Dhannā's threat worked. Saunjhiyā had to appear in his real form.

Gopāla and Kṛṣṇaprema (Ronald Nixon)

An interesting example of the sacred image's reciprocation in love is found in the relationship between Kṛṣṇaprema and Gopāla, the image of his guru Yaśodā Mā, whom he served as a *pūjārī* (ritual worshiper).[1] Yaśodā Mā had motherly affection for the image Gopāla and she was for Gopāla his dear mother. This is evident from a particular episode which Yaśodā Mā related to Dilip Roy, the noted musician, writer, and devotee, in answer to a question. Dilip Roy said: "Mā! I have heard that the image Bālagopāla, whom Gopāler Mā, a disciple of Rāmakṛṣṇa, used to serve once complained to her that there was no pillow on his bed. She asked him to sleep on her bed resting his head on her arm as a pillow. Bālāgopāla began to sleep with her and was happy. Is that true? Do things of this kind happen in the present age?"

Mā replied: "Yes, they do. I know from my own experience. You see my image Gopāla in the almirah over there. He once came to me at night when I was asleep and said, pursing his tiny lips: 'Mā! You are sleeping comfortably, but there is no sleep for me, for the ants are biting me.' I got up with a start and saw that I had by mistake put a bottle of honey by his side and the ants had collected there. I removed the ants from his body and made him sleep on my bed. He was happy and slept soundly."[2]

Yaśodā Mā had motherly affection for Kṛṣṇaprema, too, and affectionately called him "Gopāla." Kṛṣṇaprema called her "Mā." Thus, Kṛṣṇa-

[1]Kapoor, *Saints of Vraja*, 293-311.

[2]Kapoor, *Vraja ke Bhakt*, vol. 1, 236.

prema was the elder brother (*dādā*) of the younger Gopāla.

The younger Gopāla was only too happy to accept him as his *dādā*. Once Kṛṣṇaprema lay Bālagopāla to rest at night and locked the temple from the outside. After some time he heard Bālāgopāla calling: "*Dādā, Dādā! āmā ke śīt lāgche. Janlā kholā āche, Dādā.* I am feeling cold. The window is open." Kṛṣṇaprema was overwhelmed by the affection with which Bālagopāla called him *dādā*. He reopened the temple, closed the window, and covered Bālagopāla with a quilt. When covering him he said: "*Gopāla! tomākeo śīt lāge*? Gopāla, you too feel cold?" They talked to each other in Bengali because they were both sons of a Bengali mother. But what Kṛṣṇaprema said brought tears to the eyes of Bālagopāla. Why? Because he found him deficient in the love that was expected from an elder brother. Kṛṣṇaprema's love would have been equal to love for a younger brother only if he regarded Gopāla as in every sense his younger brother, who depends on him for care and protection. If he entertained any doubt about this, his love was bound to fall short of that expectation. Kṛṣṇaprema's question had betrayed his ignorance of the real nature of the younger brother and love for him.

Bālagopāla had fully reciprocated the feeling of Yaśodā Mā. It was in accordance with his reciprocation of her feeling for him that he called Kṛṣṇaprema *dādā*.

Bhagavān fully reciprocates the feelings of the devotee, but if the devotee does not fully reciprocate Bhagavān's feelings, Bhagavān feels hurt.

Gopīnātha and Govinda Ghoṣa

A typical example of the *bhakti* of parental love is found in Govinda Ghoṣa, a companion of Śrī Caitanya Mahāprabhu. Govinda Ghoṣa was simple in heart and dear to Mahāprabhu. While Mahāprabhu was traveling from Nīlācala to Bengal, Govinda Ghoṣa was one of the millions of people who accompanied him. One day, after Mahāprabhu had eaten his food, he asked Govinda to give him a *harītakī*[3] to clean his mouth. Govinda went to a nearby village and brought two *harītakīs*. One he gave to Mahāprabhu, the other he kept for the next day. The next day, when Mahāprabhu again asked for *harītakī*, Govinda immediately gave him the other. Mahāprabhu said: "Govinda! It seems you stored a *harī-*

[3]The fruit of the yellow myrobalan tree.

takī yesterday. Since you have the tendency to store you are not fit for the life of a renunciant. Go home and live the life of a householder." Govinda was stunned. Tears streamed out of his eyes. Mahāprabhu then caressed him and said: "Govinda! You are not at fault. I myself sat in your heart and prompted you to store the *harītakī*. You know why? I have to teach renunciant Vaiṣṇavas that the tendency to store is baneful. Besides, I have to show through you how far the benign Lord can go to fulfill the desire of the devotee who surrenders to him. But you must not be sorry because you lose my company. I shall come to you and never leave again."

Govinda went and began to live and practice private worship (*bhajana*) in a cottage on the bank of the Gaṅgā in Agradvīpa. One day he was sitting on the bank of the Gaṅgā meditating on Mahāprabhu when a wave splashed over him and brought with it what looked like a burned piece of wood. He put the wood aside and again began to meditate. In meditation he heard Mahāprabhu say: "Govinda! Pick up and keep carefully in your cottage the object you think is a burned log of wood." Govinda could not understand Mahāprabhu's purpose. The next morning he was surprised to see that what had appeared like burned wood was a black stone.

One day Mahāprabhu arrived at Govinda's cottage along with some of his companions. He said to him: "Govinda! Did you get the stone?"

"Yes, Mahāprabhu. I got it," said Govinda.

Mahāprabhu said: "Tomorrow I shall install an image made from that stone."

The next day came, God knows from where, a sculptor who made an image from the stone within a short time. Mahāprabhu installed the image with his own hand and called it Gopīnātha. He said to Govinda: "Govinda! Didn't I tell you that I shall come to you and never leave again? I shall live with you in the form of this image. Now marry and serve this image."

Govinda married. His wife died after giving birth to a son. The son was now five years old. Govinda imagined Gopīnātha also to be a child of five and felt parental affection towards him. He sometimes neglected his son and served Gopīnātha, sometimes neglected Gopīnātha and served his son. After some time his son died. Govinda was greatly aggrieved. He was angry with Gopīnātha for he thought he had taken his son away. He gave up food and drink and lay before Gopīnātha in protestation. He also did not offer anything to Gopīnātha to eat.

At night Gopīnātha said to Govinda: "Pitājī (father)! I have been hungry since this morning. You have not given me even a drop of water. Why are you punishing me for no fault of mine? If a man has two sons and providence takes one away, should the other be made to starve? You have lost one son. It is natural that you should be bereaved, but why kill me?"

Govinda said: "Lord! You took away my son. Your heart did not weep for me. Still you call me: Pitājī, Pitājī! Is that not sheer hypocrisy?"

Govinda's anger had for the time being eclipsed his parental affection for Gopīnātha. Therefore, he said this to him in his capacity as Bhagavān, not as his son. In reciprocation he replied as Bhagavān: "Govinda! I tell you one secret. I cannot be the son of a father who has two sons. It was all well as long as you were my father and I was your son. When you had another son, how could I be your son? Now do not grieve for your other son, because he is freed from bondage. Look at me and forget your grief. Am I not your son?"

"You are, but will you perform my post-mortem offerings?" asked Govinda in anger.

Gopīnātha replied in a soft voice: "Why not? Post-mortem offerings are darkened acts (*rājasika*).[4] But you are my father. If you desire that your son should perform your post-mortem offerings, I promise that I shall perform them."

Then Govinda was pleased. He cooked food, offered it to Gopīnātha, and himself took the grace-remains.

After some time Govinda died. Gopīnātha wept. Tears were seen trickling down his cheeks. At night he said to the new priest: "Govinda was my father. I shall perform his post-mortem offerings. I shall be impure[5] for a month. During this period I shall eat only boiled rice with clarified butter and wear clothes that are appropriate to the occasion. After one month I shall perform the post-mortem offerings in front of everyone according to the rules laid down in the scriptures and I shall offer the funeral cakes with my own hand. You do everything as I say."

The news spread like wild fire that on the Dark Ekādaśī (the eleventh day after the full moon) of the month of Caitra (March-April), Gopīnātha would perform the post-mortem offerings of his father Govinda Ghoṣa.

---

[4]That is, they are woven predominantly from the material thread (*guṇa*) of *rajas* which means dusty, unclear, as when the air is filled with dust and one cannot see clearly. It is a mid-quality between *sattva*, clarity, and *tamas*, darkness, opacity. [Ed.]

[5]Impure because of the death of a close relative, according to Hindu belief and practice.

Many people gathered at the place of the rites. Gopīnātha was carried there duly dressed for the ceremony. He performed the ceremony before everyone. People wept to see the Lord's affection for his devotee and his utmost concern for the fulfillment of his wish. Even now every year on that day Gopīnātha of Agradvīpa performs the post-mortem offerings of his father.

Gopāla and Durgī Mā

Durgī Mā[6] worshiped her sacred image Gopāla. She had motherly affection for him. She was his affectionate mother, he her affectionate child. Both lived happily in seclusion in a cottage of Raṅgajī's Temple in Vṛndāvana. Both had forgotten the world on account of their love for each other. Durgī Mā's world had shrunk to the tiny feet of her little Gopāla. Gopāla's world had shrunk to the lap of his affectionate mother. His reciprocation for her feeling was complete and natural.

Durgī Mā was now very old. She said to Gopāla one day: "Gopāla, you should now serve me, because it is not possible for me to serve you."

Gopāla was only too happy to hear this. He started serving her with all his heart and soul. Mā sat quietly shedding tears of love as she watched him serving her. He not only served her but also kept the house neat and clean by sweeping it carefully.

One day came Shyāmā Devī, a lady who was intensely devoted to Durgī Mā, and said: "Mā, your house used to be so dirty, but now I find it so clean. Who cleans it?"

"Who else will except Gopāla?" replied Mā in her simple and unsophisticated way.

Gopāla served his mother well. But he also teased her at times, because it was his nature to tease.

Mā never begged for anything from anyone. She depended on what people gave her on their own. One day she had no provisions at all. She said to Gopāla: "Gopāla, today I do not have anything to offer you. You go and eat at the house of some *gopī* (cowherd woman)."

Only Gopāla knows which *gopī* he blessed that day. But when he returned after eating, he sat on the verandah outside while Mā waited and wept for him inside.

---

[6]Kapoor, *Vraja ke Bhakt*, vol. 1, 132-45.

In the meantime, the wife of the *mahanta* (leader) of the Raṅgajī Temple happened to come. She was surprised to see that the door of Durgī Mā's room was closed, while Gopāla was lying in the cradle outside. She pushed the door open and saw that Mā was sitting still and shedding tears of anxiety. She said: "Mā! Why have you turned Gopāla out?"

"What? Has he come?" asked Mā with a start. She went out hurriedly and hugged him. Both mother and son enjoyed the hug. Was it for the purpose of enjoying the hug, the union after separation, that Gopāla remained outside? Gopāla alone knows, though it is true that he is fond of appearing to his devotees and then disappearing to enhance the bliss of union after separation.

Once Durgī Mā went to Govardhana for circumambulation with her Gopāla. On her head in a basket she kept some clothes and on them Gopāla was comfortably seated. From time to time she lowered the basket to see whether Gopāla was there or not because Gopāla was restive and it was not in his nature to stay in one place for long. When she returned home after the circumambulation, she put the basket aside and tried to unlock her room, but the lock would not open. She thought she would wait on the verandah with Gopāla until someone came whom she could ask to open the lock. But when she looked into the basket she was aghast to find that Gopāla was not there. She began to weep and wail.

At that time Śrī Manohara Dāsa Bābā of Veṇukuñja was somewhere nearby. He recognized the cry of Durgī Mā and hastened to her. Mā narrated her woeful plight to him as she wept and wept. Manohara Bābā tried to console her. He also tried to open the lock. It opened. As he pushed open the door he saw Gopāla sleeping there in his cradle. He shouted: "Mā! Your Gopāla is here. You locked him in and forgot. You are now needlessly blaming him and crying."

Someone else would have thought that the old woman had gone mad. But Manohara Bābā knew that Gopāla was mischievous and fond of pranks.

Mā was filled with delight and anger. She would have scolded Gopāla for teasing her, but she saw him fast asleep. So she refrained and her anger subsided.

Was Gopāla actually asleep? Perhaps not. For otherwise, how could he enjoy the *rasa* (flavor) of his mother's unusual mood of delight mixed with anger?

Who was Durgī Mā you may ask? You need only know that she was the mother of Gopāla and Gopāla was her child. But if you feel more curious about her you may be told that she was born in 1858 in the house of a goldsmith in the village of Mīrāpura Sindaḍe in Jammū. She was devotionally inclined even while she was a child. She used to assist her grandmother in the service of her sacred image and chant the holy names like her for hours. She was married at the age of thirteen. Tormented constantly for seventeen years by her husband and mother-in-law on account of her religious leanings, she sneaked out of home one night. She earned her living by working as a cook or maidservant at Lahore, Dehradun, and Haridvāra. But her religious cultivation continued and it became more and more intense. Ultimately it became impossible for her to do any work. Then she came to Vṛndāvana, lived for some time in Jagannātha's temple, and then moved to her room in the temple of Raṅgajī.

She was always lost in the thought and service of Gopāla. Her eyes always swam in tears of love. The slightest stimulants of the sport of Kṛṣṇa sent her into ecstasy. While bathing in the waters of the Yamunā she often had visions of Kṛṣṇa playing there with the milkmaids and she would lose outward consciousness.

In that condition she remained standing in the Yamunā for hours. Even if a tortoise bit her she remained unconscious. Once she heard the sound of someone's flute near Sevākuñja and fell unconscious. She remained unconscious for eight hours. She was often seen falling unconscious in the talks about Kṛṣṇa of Śrī Gaurāṅga Dāsa Bābā.

Usually she sat inside her room with the doors closed and repeated the holy names. Sometimes people stood near the door to hear her chanting. They could distinctly hear two voices. One was the voice of Durgī Mā with which they were familiar. The other was the sweet and tender voice of a child. Who could that child be except Gopāla? Once a lady heard her saying to Gopāla: "Gopāla listen. The sound of the holy names is coming out of every pore of my body."

Durgī Mā did not usually speak about her spiritual experiences. But she sometimes spoke about them to one or two persons who were close to her. Once she said to deputy collector Janārdana Dāsa: "I have thrice had a vision of the celestial Vṛndāvana."

But towards the later period of her life it appeared that she always lived in the celestial Vṛndāvana. Her room was not built of the material of this world. It was a beautiful arbor of celestial Vṛndāvana in which lotuses grew all around, the peacocks danced, the black-bees buzzed and cuckoos sang.

One day as Śyāmā Devī entered her room, she said: "Slowly, come around this side."

"What's the matter?" asked Śyāmā Devī.

"Don't you see the lotuses blooming on that side?" replied Durgī Mā.

Śyāmā Devī did not see the lotuses. Anyone else in her place would have thought that Durgī Mā's vision was illusory. But Śyāmā Devī knew that her own vision was defective, not Durgī Mā's.

One day Durgī Mā said to Śyāmā Devī: "Gopāla has become very mischievous. You know what he said to me the other day? He said: 'Mā! You wear a silken *sārī* and put vermilion on your head. I shall marry you.'"

Śyāmā Devī laughed and said: "What is wrong with that? I can bring a silken *sārī*."

"Does it become him to propose marriage with his mother?" burst out Durgī Mā in anger.

But who was really at fault, Mā or Gopāla? Was it not the love of Mā that had made Gopāla what he was? He was a child. His ways could not but be childish. Gopāla would have been at fault if he had not fully reciprocated her parental (motherly) love.

Durgī Mā's attachment to the celestial Vṛndāvana gradually increased and her attachment to terrestrial Vṛndāvana decreased. On August 5, 1977, at the age of 119, she left the terrestial Vṛndāvana and entered the celestial.

Raṅganātha and Āṇḍāla

Āṇḍāl nurtured erotic feeling towards Bhagavān Raṅganātha. She worshiped him as her husband. Raṅganātha did not lag behind in reciprocation. He accepted her as his wife. The narrative of Āṇḍāl's story is as follows:

In the ninth century there lived in Villipūtur, a town about forty miles south-west of Madhurai in South India, a Vaiṣṇava whose name was Viṣṇucitta, but who was commonly known as Periyālvār or the "Great Ālvār," because of his devotion which was proverbial. He had a garden in which he grew *tulasī* and fragrant flowers. He made garlands from the flowers of the garden for the famous Nārāyaṇa image of the town, whom he worshiped as Kṛṣṇa. One day he was digging a pit in the garden so that he might bury the rubbish composed of the wild plants that had grown there. He had dug only a little when he was astonished to see a golden image lying under the earth. As he removed the earth he found that the image was the living image of a new-born child, a girl, who surpassed in beauty anything he had seen before. He brought her home and started bringing her up with care and attention.

The girl was regarded as the incarnation of Bhū Devī (Goddess Earth), one of the three manifestations of Mahālakṣmī, who was born out of earth for Viṣṇucitta just as Sītā was born out of earth for Janaka. She was named Godā, but later she began to be called Āṇḍāl.

As a manifestation of Mahālakṣmī, her love for Nārāyaṇa, whom like her father she worshiped as Kṛṣṇa, was natural. When she came of age, she began to love him passionately as her husband. She depicted her love in Tāmil poems which form a part of the Four Thousand Divine Verses (*Nālāyir Divya-prabandham*) regarded as the Tāmil Veda by Śrī Vaiṣṇavas.

Āṇḍāl continued to worship Kṛṣṇa as her lover. The goal of her spiritual cultivation was marriage with Kṛṣṇa.

In one of her poems she said: "O Lord of Dvārakā! Ever since I came of age my breasts have been craving for you. They have swelled up and I have resolved that they are only for you. I have been worshiping you so that you may come quickly. Will you?"

Āṇḍāl used to wear the garlands, woven by her father for the deity, in her hair, put a gold necklace around her neck, redden her lips and look into the mirror and say: "Am I not as beautiful as my lord? Will he not be pleased to marry me?"

One day Viṣṇucitta happened to notice this. He said angrily: "Girl! Have you always been doing this?" He did not adorn the image with a garland that day. At night the image said to him in dream: "You serve me with a garland every day. Why did you not bring the garland today?"

Viṣṇucitta replied: "My lord! The garland was worn by my daughter. It became polluted. How could I offer a polluted garland to you?"

"Polluted? How can a garland become polluted if it is worn by her? It becomes even more fragrant, more purified. Listen, from tomorrow I shall not wear a garland that is not worn and sanctified by her." Viṣṇucitta was petrified. "Has the Goddess Bhū or Śrī really manifested herself in the form of my daughter?" he wondered.

Now Viṣṇucitta wanted to arrange his daughter's marriage. He began to look for a suitable person to whom she could be married. But he knew that she would marry Kṛṣṇa and no one else. For, though not yet married, she had begun to think that she belonged to Śrī Raṅganātha of Śrīraṅgam, whom she worshiped as Kṛṣṇa and no one else. She always thought of him, talked of him, dreamed of him. It was impossible for her to live even for a moment without thinking of him.

Viṣṇucitta not only had no objection to her marriage to Raṅganātha, he would have felt blessed if Raṅganātha married her. But was that possible? Was ever a girl, howsoever devoted, married to a sacred image? The thought always disturbed him. He did not know what to do.

But could Raṅganātha remain a passive observer, a heartless lover? Āṇḍāl's love had created a craving for her in his heart. If Āṇḍāl could not live without him, how could he live without her? He appeared before Viṣṇucitta in a dream and said: "Viṣṇucitta, do not worry. What you think is impossible will happen. I shall soon marry your daughter."

The same day he said to his chief priest in a dream: "Go to Villipūtur with my umbrellas, flags, musicians, elephants, horses and all my retinue and bring Āṇḍāl to me. For I shall marry her."

So they went and brought Āṇḍāl in a palanquin covered with curtains with the uninterrupted sounds of musical instruments of various kinds and proclamations that befitted the auspicious occasion. They entered the bride-groom's sacred hall (the outer sanctum) and removed the curtains from the palanquin.

The marriage was duly performed according to the Gandharva rites in the inner sanctum. Though the Gandharva marriage is performed by a man and a woman in secret, in this marriage Viṣṇucitta, his disciple Vallabhadevan and many others were present.

At the conclusion of the marriage everyone saw Āṇḍāl, dressed in a silken *sārī*, her hair bedecked with flowers, bracelets tinkling and eyes darting from side to side like fish, step up to the bride-groom's bed, the multifaced cobra, embrace his feet and disappear.[7]

Giridhara Gopāla and Mīrā

Mīrā was the grand-daughter of Dūdājī, the king of Meḍtā and the daughter-in-law of Mahārānā Sāṅgā, the ruler of Mārwāḍ and the most powerful Hindu ruler of his time. She was born with strong propen-

---

[7] Rasikamohana Vidyābhūṣaṇa, *Śrī Vaiṣṇava*, 60-77.

sities (*saṃskāras*)[8] for *bhakti*. She was only a child when this became apparent. At that time a holy man came to her palace. He had with him his sacred image Giridhara Gopāla. Mīrā felt very attracted towards the image. When the holy man was about to leave she insisted that he leave the image with her. Why should the holy man leave the image with a child to be toyed with by her? He speeded up his departure and carried the image with him. Mīrā became very sad. She would not eat or drink or play. She only shed tears. She did not know what had happened to her. But Giridhara Gopāla knew what had happened to her. She had fallen in love with him. How could he remain unaffected? He became equally sad. He said to the holy man in a dream: "Mīrā has stolen my heart. You must go back and leave me with her." The holy man had to obey. Mīrā was happy to find Gopāla and Gopāla to find Mīrā. They began to live together happily. Mīrā served Gopāla as best as she could, or, shall we say, played with him as she liked, because at that age she hardly had any idea of ritual service. But how did it matter to Gopāla whether it was service or play so long as he liked it? And he liked it, because Mīrā did it all in love.

One day Mīrā saw a marriage party passing in front of her palace. She became curious about the bridegroom. She asked her mother: "Mā, who is he?"

"He is the bridegroom. He is going to marry."

"Mā, I shall also marry. Where is my bridegroom?"

"Your bridegroom is Giridhara Gopāla. You are already married to him," replied her mother to rid herself of Mīrā's childish insistence on marriage.

Mīrā was happy to know this. She said to Gopāla: "Gopāla, you are my husband." Gopāla said in her heart: "Yes. I am your husband for ever and ever."

When Mīrā came of age, her people wanted to get her married. She protested. How could she marry anyone else, when she was already married to Gopāla? Though the marriage was not solemnized by a ceremony outside, it was solemnized in the hearts of Mīrā and Gopāla. But the elders must arrange her marriage. It would be disgraceful for them if she remained unmarried. So she was married to prince Bhojarāja, the eldest son of Rānā Sāṅgā.

---

[8]Impressions, desires, believed to be left in the mind by past actions and experiences. [Ed.]

Mīrā's cultivation of *bhakti* continued unabated even in her father-in-law's house. She had carried her Giridhara Gopāla with her. Most of her time she spent in his service in various ways. She was a poetess. She composed poems, sang them before Giridhara Gopāla and danced. Her *bhakti* was admired by her husband. Unfortunately, Bhojarāja died in 1523, seven years after the marriage. Rānā Sāṅgā built a separate temple of Giridhara Gopāla near the temple of Kumbha Shyāmā in Chittor, so that Mīrā might pursue her cultivation undisturbed in that temple. He always took special care of her. But he also died fighting against Bābar in 1527. His younger son Ratan Sinha ascended the throne. Four years later he also died. He was succeeded by his younger brother Vikramājita.

With the ascent of Vikramājita to the throne began a period of trials and tribulations for Mīrā. Mīrā was now so deeply in love with Giridhara Gopāla that she could not for a moment live without him. But he appeared and disappeared as is his wont. In moments of separation she found some relief in the company of holy men who visited her in the temple and in singing and dancing in the temple. Vikramājita asked her not to associate with the holy men and dance, because that was not in keeping with her dignity and it brought disgrace to the royal family. He asked his sister Ūdā Bāi and others in the family to persuade her to give up her ways. But all their warnings and importunities failed to persuade her. She became all the more firm in her *bhakti*. She sang:

If Rāṇā is displeased
Let him be.
I shall leave his domain.
Elsewhere shall I go.
If Giridhara is displeased
Where shall I go?

Rānā insisted on her following his instructions. He appointed servants and maid-servants to watch her activities and report if she behaved otherwise. Someone reported to him that she practiced *bhakti* during the day, but at night she enjoyed the company of some man inside her room, with whom he had heard her talking. Rānā was wild with rage. At night he went to her room with a sword in hand and stood at the door. He actually heard her talking to someone. He knocked hard at the door. When Mīrā opened the door, he was surprised to see that no one was there except her.

"To whom were you talking?" he shouted.

"To whom shall I talk except my Gopāla," she replied.

He felt humiliated and went back.

He thought the root cause of Mīrā's intransigence was Gopāla. So he had him stolen one day. But who can steal him, who steals not only the possessions but also the hearts of men? He left the place where he had been hidden and stepped onto his seat on the altar of Mīrā's temple.

This should have opened the eyes of the Rānā. It is strange that it did not. He thought that if Gopāla could not be separated from Mīrā, he must separate Mīrā from Gopāla forever. Therefore, he sent her a cobra in a basket, under the pretext that he was sending her a Śālagrāma stone. But as Mīrā opened the basket what she saw was not the cobra, but a Śālagrāma stone with a garland.

When this also failed the Rānā sent her a cup of poison under the pretext of foot-wash-nectar (*caraṇāmṛta*).[9] Mīrā came to know that it was poison. But because she was told that it was foot-wash-nectar, she drank it happily as foot-wash-nectar sent to her by her Lord. She drank and danced in ecstasy. The poison had actually turned into foot-wash-nectar.

A devotee disregards the difficulties that come in his way. He places his foot on them considering them to be the rungs of a ladder for climbing up and goes on climbing upwards. Kṛṣṇa always helps him do so. So with each obstacle that the Rānā put in her way Mīrā went on climbing upwards. Each intensified her devotion.

Ultimately she became impatient to leave the unpleasant world and join Kṛṣṇa forever. In her impatience she rushed to Vṛndāvana, stopping at Meḍtā for a while and taking from there her friend Lalitā as her companion.

As soon as she reached Vṛndāvana, the land of her Lord, she heaved a sigh of relief. Her heart was filled with joy to see Vṛndāvana, the Yamunā, the forests, the birds and animals, the trees and creepers, all pulsating with love for Kṛṣṇa, because, she thought, they always enjoy his proximity and vision, his healing touch, his soothing words and the maddening notes of his flute. She thought that she would also find him soon. She went from place to place, from forest to forest and from temple to temple, to find and embrace him. But he only appeared and

[9] Water used to wash the feet of the sacred images, gurus, and saints. It is considered a source of great spiritual blessing. Devotees drink a little bit when they visit temples and holy people.

disappeared or smiled at her from a distance, but never came close to her.

He did not, because the kind of relationship, in which she had pledged herself to him, the conjugal relationship as between husband and wife, was not possible in Vṛndāvana. Vṛndāvana was the land of love, which was pure, spontaneous and sublime, which was above the Vedic sanctions of morality and immorality, above the rites and rituals of matrimonial alliances or anything that involved constraints and checked its spontaneous flow.

Mīrā was disappointed. She did not know what to do. She wanted to meet Śrī Jīva Gosvāmin for advice. Śrī Jīva refused to meet her, because, he said, he was a male (*puruṣa*) and he did not meet with women (*prakṛti*). Mīrā retorted through someone: "I had thought that in Vṛndāvana there was only one male and all the rest were female. I am now surprised to find that there is at least one more male here." Jīva was pleased and allowed her to meet him.

Perhaps Śrī Jīva explained to her why it was not possible for the Kṛṣṇa of Vṛndāvana to respond to her feeling, because in Vṛndāvana he did not marry and responded only to *rāgātmikā bhakti* or passionate *bhakti*, such as that of the cowherd girls of Vṛndāvana, which is based wholly on *rāga* or pure love and did not stand in need of being solemnized by the ritual of marriage. He must have also told her that her craving could be satisfied only by the Kṛṣṇa of Dvārakā, who could easily add to the harem of sixteen thousand, one hundred and eight queens, whom he married, one more if he was so pleased.

So Mīrā went to Dvārakā. The Dvārakādhīśa (King of Dvārakā) was already impatiently waiting for her. She went and stood before him. At first, she could not say anything, because her heart was full. She only shed tears. Slowly her heart began to throb and feet began to move. She began to dance in ecstasy and sing as she danced:

> My Lord! How I have cherished
> So long to meet and serve you.
> But you have come and gone
> and never stayed very long
> I cannot suffer separation anymore.
> I have lost my hunger, lost my sleep
> My body has become lean.
> Life hangs by a thread.

I have come to you,
Never to leave again.
Do not turn me away
For I shall die.
If I die, what will you gain?
You will only tarnish your name.
So, My Lord! Have mercy on me,
Have mercy on me.

As she sang and danced a light flashed out of the body of Dvārakādhīśa. Mīrā disappeared[10] with it. Dvārakādhīśa drew her into his own self and let a piece of her *sārī* remain hanging from his mouth[11] to show that she had attained the goal of her life—eternal union in love with the Lord.

Śrī Viśvanātha Cakravartin and the Mañjarī Identity

āṇḍāl and Mīrā had the particular type of erotic love towards Kṛṣṇa that is called *svakīya*. In *svakīya* love the relationship between the lover and the beloved is solemnized by marriage duly performed according to the rites prescribed by the scriptures. There is another type of love called *parakīya* in which the relationship is not solemnized by marriage. Śrī Rūpa defines a *parakīyā* heroine as one who offers herself to Kṛṣṇa on account of her *rāga* or natural attachment towards him, without entering into formal wedlock and without caring for the propriety or impropriety of the act according to the scriptures. There is still another type of erotic love called *mañjarī* love, in which the *parakīyā* heroine offers herself primarily to Rādhā, and only secondarily to Kṛṣṇa. Her love towards Rādhā is the permanent component (*sthāyin*) and her love towards Kṛṣṇa is the transitory or auxiliary component (*sañcarin*) of her love.

The specialty of the *mañjarī*'s love is its purity. The *mañjarī* cannot even think of having a bodily relationship with Kṛṣṇa. She is always lost in pure, selfless service of Rādhā and Kṛṣṇa. On account of the purity of her love she has free entrance into the bower where Rādhā and Kṛṣṇa meet secretly and where the girlfriends (*sakhis*) cannot go. She also enjoys the special privilege of serving them in their amorous sports.

---

[10]She disappeared in 1603.
[11]That piece is preserved in the temple even now.

If Rādhā pretends to be angry in love because Kṛṣṇa has broken his promise to her or committed some other fault, the *mañjarī*, on account of her exclusive devotion to Rādhā and the purity of her love, is also in the privileged position of admonishing and scolding Kṛṣṇa for his fault and standing as sentinel at Rādhā's bower to prevent his entry.

Kṛṣṇa cannot but reciprocate the love of the *mañjarī*. He does not crave bodily relationship with her. He has the highest regard for her on account of her purity and selfless service to Rādhā. When Rādhā is displeased with him, on account of some fault of his, he not only allows himself to be scolded by the *mañjarī*, but cajoles and flatters and begs her to persuade Rādhā to give up her anger and bring about his meeting with her.

The form of worship of the *mañjarī* was for the first time introduced by Śrī Caitanya Mahāprabhu. It has been practiced by his followers. This is apparent from the hymns and prayers of Śrī Rūpa,[12] Śrī Raghunātha Dāsa,[13] Śrī Prabodhānanda,[14] Śrī Narottama Dāsa Ṭhākura,[15] and others.

A glimpse of the worship entailed in the love of the *mañjarī* is found in an episode relating to Śrī Viśvanātha Cakravartin, the great Gauḍīya teacher,[16] who is regarded as the incarnation of Śrī Rūpa. Once he entered into a debate with the scholars of some other community on the *parakīya* doctrine, of which he was an enthusiastic exponent. He made them speechless by arguments and quotations from the *Bhāgavata, Padma, Sanatkumāra Saṃhitā*, and other scriptures. The scholars felt humiliated. They hatched a plan to kill him. With this purpose one morning they went to the place where he used to go for a walk. They did not see him, but they saw a girl who was picking flowers with her companions. They asked her: "Lālī, have you seen Cakravarti?"

"I did see him, but I do not know where he has disappeared," replied the girl with a smile.

The scholars were charmed by the beauty and luster of her face and her graceful smile and demeanor. Out of curiosity they asked her again: "Lālī, whose daughter are you? Where do you live?"

The girl said: "I am a companion of Rādhā. She is just now in her

---

[12] *Ujjvala-nīlamaṇi, Sakhi-prakaraṇa*, 133.
[13] *Vraja-vilāsa-stava*, 39.
[14] *Vṛndāvana-mahimāmṛta*, 16.64.
[15] *Prema-bhakti-candrikā*.
[16] He was born in 1654 C.E.

father-in-law's house in Yāvaṭ. She has sent me to pick flowers for Kṛṣṇa.

As soon as the girl said this, she disappeared and the scholars saw in her place Śrī Viśvanātha Cakravartin himself. The scholars realized that *parakīya* love was real and Viśvanātha Cakravartin was accomplished (*siddha*) in the worship through the love of the *mañjarī* as a mode of *parakīya* love.

One might doubt the reality of the *mañjarī* form, specially in the case of a male practitioner. For how can a practitioner be at once male and female? It must be emphasized in this connection that the spiritual world is a world of feeling (*bhāva*). The spiritual body is not physical and it is not male or female in the physical sense. It is made of feeling or love (*bhāva-deha*). Feeling itself assumes a figure. The figure is according to the feeling. It is neither physical nor imaginary. It is real, for feeling (*bhāva*) is the essence of the pleasuring-giving power (*hlādinī-śakti*) of the Lord, which includes within itself the existence-giving power (*sandhinī-śakti*) which is the basis of all existence, including the existence of Bhagavān.

Sacred Images and the Feelings of the *Bhakta*

Deity (*ṭhākura*) has been found to reciprocate the feelings of the *bhakta* even in the form of the sacred image.

Gopāla Bhaṭṭa Gosvāmin used to worship the Śālagrāma stone. Once he wished that if his object of worship had a human form, he could also dress and decorate him in various ways like the other *bhaktas*. The same night the stone changed its form and stood up in the form of the beautiful sacred image of Rādhāramaṇa, the form in which we see him today.

Śrī Gadādhara Paṇḍita, a companion of Śrī Caitanya Mahāprabhu, used to worship the big image of Toṭā Gopīnātha in standing posture in Purī. When he became old it became difficult for him to worship him in that posture. Gopīnātha realized his difficulty and sat down. Even today we see him sitting unlike other sacred images.

Pisī Mā Gosvāminī used to worship Murāri Gupta's images of Gaura and Nitāi in their temple in Vṛndāvana. When she became a hundred years old and could not worship them anymore, she entrusted their service to Gopeśvara Gosvāmin. Gopeśvara Gosvāmin's feeling towards the images was of the friendly type. He wanted to serve them to his utmost satisfaction according to his feeling. But since the images were small in size and looked more like Child Gaurāṅga and Child Nitāi they suited the parental feeling of Pisī Mā, but not his friendly feeling. He told Pisī Mā that the small sized images failed to arouse his friendly sentiments, therefore he could not serve them with satisfaction. Pisī Mā solved his difficulty. She entered the temple, took hold of the chins of the Gaura and Nitāi with her hands and pulled them up. They allowed themselves to be pulled and assumed their present forms, which are taller.

There is a temple of Sākṣī Gopāla near Purī. A queen, who was intensely devoted to him, had a precious pearl. She wished that Sākṣī Gopāla had a hole in his nose to wear a *bulāka*, a kind of nose ornament, made from the pearl. How beautiful, she thought, he would look with the ornament. She felt sorry that her wish could not be fulfilled. At night Sākṣī Gopāla appeared to her in dream and said: "Why be sorrowful? See. My nose has a hole. My mother did it when I was a child." The next morning when she went to the temple she saw that the image actually had a hole in its nose exactly at the point where the *bulāka* is worn.

The deity always reciprocates the wish of his pure-hearted devotee. The reciprocation is not willed; it is spontaneous.

Verification of the Law of Subjugation

Kṛṣṇa is subjugated by *bhakti* and enjoys that subjugation. He controls everything, but likes to be controlled by the devotees. He accepts the service of his devotees and relishes it, but he relishes serving them more than being served by them. There is no service, howsoever mean or contemptible, which he will not do for them. In the Rājasūya sacrifice of Yudhiṣṭhira he took upon himself the task of washing the feet of the guests and cleaning their plates after the festival. In the battle of the *Mahābhārata* he chose to be the charioteer of Arjuna and the groom of his horses. He served not only Arjuna, but also his horses whom he rubbed, fed, and tended. Examples of Bhagavān's subjugation by devotees of our own times and the services he rendered to them are also not less startling.

Examples

Bhagavān as Barber Sena and Rāja Vīrasiṃha

In Bhāndhavagarha, a town in Baghela Khaṇḍa, there lived Sena, the barber.[1] Although a barber by profession, he was a great devotee and he spent most of his time in the service of the Lord and the Vaiṣṇavas. He also used to serve Rāja Vīrasiṃha, the ruler of the place, as a masseur. One day when he was about to go to the Rāja to give him a massage, some saints came to his house who wanted shaves. He could not turn

[1] Nābhājī, *Bhakta-māla*, 63.

them away. He became busy with serving and entertaining them and forgot all about his service to the king.

The Rāja would have been mighty angry with him, if he was kept waiting for long. The Lord did not want any harm to come to his devotee. He, therefore, went himself in the guise of Sena, the barber, to the Rāja and started massaging him. The Rāja found the massage that day much more comforting and soothing than on other days.

After the holy men were duly served Sena started for the Rāja's palace. The Rāja was surprised to see him. "What brings you again?" he asked. Sena did not understand what he meant. He only said prayerfully: "Excuse me Rāja Sāhib for coming late today."

"What do you mean? Have you not already massaged me?" said the king.

Sena stood bewildered. Both he and the king understood that someone else in the guise of Sena had come and gone after giving the massage. Who could he be except the one who alone could play Sena with such perfection, whose heart alone would beat to think of the plight of Sena and his possible chastisement by the king, who alone could take so much trouble to save Sena from the wrath of the king?

A sudden change came upon the king. He took initiation from Sena and served him and his Lord all the rest of his life. This was bound to be, because he had received the touch of the hand divine.

Bhagavān as Parasarāma Khātī and Rāja Jayamala

Parasarāmajī Khātī (the carpenter) was a great devotee of Śrī Rāma.[2] He was born in the village of Kalarū in the district of Nāgaura of Rājasthāna in 1462 and died in 1624 at the age of 162. He was a disciple of the famous Pīpājī, the king of Gāgarauna Garha in Rājasthāna, who renounced the world and became one of the foremost disciples of ācārya Rāmānanda.

Once Rāja Jayamala of Meḍtā was traveling in a chariot to Jodhpur. Ṭhākura Lakṣmaṇa Sinha of Lāvāna was with him. On the way, one of the wheels of the chariot broke. Jayamala sent for Parasarāma to repair it. Parasarāma came with his tools and made a new wheel. When the chariot started off people saw that the new wheel was moving without touching the ground. They pointed it out to Rāja Jayamala. He got

[2]Kapoor, *Nava-bhakta-māla*, 236-8.

down from his chariot and was also surprised to see the wheel moving without touching the ground. On examining the wheel closely he found that it had no joint or nail in it, as if it was made skillfully from a single piece of wood. Jayamala called Parasarāma again. He said to him: "Parasarāma, you will have to make three more wheels like the one you have just made."

Parasarāma was stupefied, because he had never come to make the wheel in the first place. But he did not take long to understand who had made it. He said: "Mahārāja, excuse me. I could not come because I was busy all the time serving some saints, whom Rāmajī had kindly sent to me. Also, I cannot make a wheel of this type. No one can, except the one who makes and unmakes the universe. You are fortunate that he came and made it for you."

"What do you say, Parasarāma? I saw you making the wheel with my own eyes."

"You must have seen me, Mahārāja. But I do not lie when I say that I did not make the wheel. You can ask the saints in whose service I remained busy at that time. I did not for a moment leave them."

"Then it must have been Śrī Rāma who came in your place. You have by your *bhakti* subjugated him to the extent that he goes and works for you when you cannot. So you kindly request him on my behalf to give me a vision. Since he has already shown mercy to me by appearing before me in disguise and making a wheel for my chariot, I cannot now rest without seeing him undisguised."

"Mahārāja, you know that Rāmajī is absolutely free. No one can make him do anything against his will."

"No. He is not. He is wholly subservient to his devotees. He cannot go against their will. If you do not pray to him for me, I shall commit suicide."

Parasarāma had to pray. He said: "Prabhu, you know that the Rāja is your devotee. That is why you have served him in disguise. Now give him a sight of you undisguised. Have mercy on him, Prabhu."

Rāmajī then appeared to the Rāja. The Rāja donated 500 *bighas* of land to Parasarāma and made for him a temple of Caturbhuja Bhagavān in Kulari which still exists.

Bhagavān as Boatman and Sanehī Rāma

Sanehī Rāmajī, born in the village of Māṃṭa in Vraja in 1842, was a great devotee of Bihārījī.[3] Since Bihārījī's temple is in Vṛndāvana and Māṭa is on the other side of the Yamunā River, one has to cross the river to go from Māṭa to Vṛndāvana. Still, Sanehī Rāma went to Vṛndāvana every evening to visit Bihārījī. Neither rain nor storm would thwart him. He would have his evening meal only after having a sight of Bihārījī.

One day he remained in meditation till late at night. When the meditation was over it was 2 a.m. But he thought that night had just set in. He started out for his visit to Bihārījī. On reaching the bank of the Yamunā, he saw in the moonlight that all the boats were moored at the bank and no boatman was there. He was filled with anxiety. He thought that he had perhaps committed some offense on account of which Bihārījī did not want to see him that day.

But soon he saw a boatman coming from the other side. As he came closer he recognized him. He was the same boatman who took him across the river and brought him back every day. With a sigh of relief he stepped into the boat. When he reached the temple he found it open as usual. He had his audience with Bihārījī to his heart's content and went back to the bank. The boatman, who was waiting for him, ferried him across the river.

Disembarking from the boat he was surprised to see a number of villagers coming to bathe in the Yamunā.

He asked the boatman: "Is it morning?"

"So it is, sir. It was already two o'clock when I took you to Vṛndāvana."

"How is it that you were here so late at night?"

"Oh, sir! Don't ask about that. Yesterday I had a quarrel with my wife. So I did not go home. I lay down on the boat but could not sleep."

"But how is it that the temple of Bihārījī was open so late at night?" Sanehī Rāma began to reflect. "Was it all a dream?"

The next day, when he went for his visit at the usual time, the boatman, who took him across every day, was on the landing. He asked: "Sir, did you not go for your visit yesterday?"

"Of course I went. Have you forgotten?" said Sanehī Rāma, as he looked at him like one who was dazed.

---

[3]Baṅke Bihārī, the name of a sacred image of Śrī Kṛṣṇa in a famous temple in Vṛndāvana. This account is also given in Kapoor, *Vraja ke Bhakt*, vol. 2, 254-7.

"When did you go? I didn't see you. Someone else must have taken you across, because I went home somewhat early yesterday."

Sanehī Rāma then realized that it was Bihārījī himself who had carried him across the river in the guise of the boatman. The realization brought tears to his eyes. The eight spontaneous symptoms like trembling and sweating also began to appear on his body. He wondered and wondered why Bihārījī should have taken all that trouble for him. But there was nothing to be wondered at in this. For Bihārījī always yearns for an opportunity to serve his devotees in whatever way possible. He has no other work to do. He says:

> *mad-bhaktānāṃ vinodārthaṃ karomi vividhāḥ kriyāḥ*[4]
>
> I perform different kinds of activities only to please my devotees.

Bhagavān as Servant in the Temple of Madanamohana and Tāja Khān

Tāja Khān, a peon in the court of Karaulī, was a devout Muslim. He lived with piety and went to the mosque every day to say his prayers. He spent most of his time in reading the Koran and meditating on God. The Muslims revered him as a true Muslim, the Hindus as a pious man.

One day he was sent by the court to the temple of Madanamohana[5] in Karaulī to deliver a message to the Gosvāmin of the temple. He happened to see the image through a window of the temple. He was so struck by its beauty that he kept on looking at it for some time. After he had delivered the message through the gatekeeper he returned. But as he returned, he looked again and again at Madanamohana and Madanamohana looked at him. He went back to the court, then went home and to the mosque. Wherever he went he found the image of Madanamohana pursuing him till it was securely seated in the temple of his heart. He forgot his prayers, Kalamā and Koran. He only thought of Madanamohana, talked of Madanamohana and kept his mind's eye always fixed on him.

Tāja Khān was born a Muslim and brought up in a culture which was averse to the image worship of the Hindus. How is it that the

[4] *Padma Purāṇa*

[5] The image worshiped by Sanātana Gosvāmin, a companion of Śrī Caitanya. The image was moved from Vṛndāvana to Jaipur and then from there to Karaulī in about 1730.

image of Madanamohana captured his heart the moment he saw him? It may be because the unconscious impressions (*saṃskāras*) of a past life were revived the moment he saw Madanamohana. Or, it may be that Madanamohana himself took such a fancy to him.

When a cup is full it spills at the slightest shake. Tāja Khān's heart was now full of love for Madanamohana and often spilt in the form of poems. He once sang:

> Oh! How my heart yearns for thee,
> Unthwarted by hunger, thirst or sleep.
> O Madanamohana! Show yourself to me.
> Each moment without your sight
> Appears like an age to me.
> Your sidelong glances thrill my heart.
> Cast your glance but once at me.
> Listen, O son of Nanda, with a moonlike face,
> Tāja your servant stands begging by your gate
> For your sight and your grace.[6]

Tāja Khān could not now remain long without looking at Madanamohana. He tried to go and see him every time the temple opened. He remained standing at the gate and looking at him through the window. When the temple was closed he peeped into the temple of his heart, of which the gates always remained open, and saw Madanamohana sitting there, always looking and smiling at him.

The way of *bhakti* is sweet, yet at times beset with difficulties, trials, and tribulations. Tāja Khān also had to face them. His Muslim brethren came to know of his *bhakti* towards Madanamohana. They declared him an infidel and excommunicated him. The Gosvāmin of the temple debarred him from going to the temple and seeing Madanamohana even from the outside, because he was a Muslim. One day when he was coming up the stairs of the temple the gatekeeper pushed him down. He felt so aggrieved that for three days he did not eat anything. He did not go to the court and remained lying at home, weeping and sobbing all the time in remembrance of Madanamohana.

For three days Madanamohana also remained cheerless without seeing him. One can imagine how deeply he felt his absence from what he did on the third day. Every night, according to tradition in the temple,

[6]The orignal language of this song is Urdu.

the priest placed a silver plate full of food near the bed of Madanamohana when he went to sleep so that he might eat if he felt hungry. That day at midnight when everybody was asleep, Madanamohana got up from bed, took that plate, and in the guise of the attendant of the temple started towards the house of Tāja Khān. On reaching his house he knocked at the door. Tāja Khān opened the door. The attendant extended the plate towards Tāja Khān and said: "Gosvāmijī has sent this grace-food and said that you must come for audience at the time of the full-dress ceremony (*śṛṅgāra ārati*) tomorrow. No one will object to your coming. He has also said that when you go you should carry this plate with you.

Tāja Khān was taken aback. He kept gazing at the young attendant who seemed to have a divine luster on his face. He took the plate from the attendant's hands and said: "Has Gosvāmijī sent this? Has he really invited me to view Madanamohana?"

"Yes, yes. It is he who has sent it and he who has invited you to a viewing. Do come," said the attendant with a smile and went away.

It was all a mystery to Tāja Khān. He had never seen the attendant before. Besides, how could he believe that the Gosvāmin who had him pushed down the stairs would send him grace-food at night and insist on his going for a viewing again? He kept musing and wondering throughout the night. But he was hungry and he had to honor the grace-food. So he ate the grace-food and cleaned the plate.

In the meantime Madanamohana said to the Gosvāmin in a dream. "Tāja Khān has not eaten since you had him pushed down the steps of the temple. I have given him the plateful of food the priest kept for me so that he may eat. He will come to visit me tomorrow. Do not prevent him."

In the morning when the priest opened the altar room, he was surprised to see the silver plate missing. Trembling with fear he went to the Gosvāmin and said, "Mahārāja! Ṭhākura's silver plate has been stolen. Believe me. I kept it with the food for his enjoyment near his bed at night and locked the door of the altar room from the outside. Please do not suspect me."

"Do not worry," said the Gosvāmin. "The thief has confessed the theft. The plate will come."

Gosvāmijī went to Mahārāja Gopāla Sinhajī who was the ruler of Karaulī at the time and reported everything to him. The Mahārāja was overwhelmed with feeling to hear about Madanamohana's concern for his devotee and the trouble he took for his sake. He was also filled with love and veneration for Tāja Khān whose *bhakti* had subjugated Madanamohana to that extent.

Tāja Khān started for the temple with the plate in hand before the time of the full-dress ceremony. But he was staggering on account of fear, because he was still not sure that he had been invited by the Gosvāmin. He was apprehensive that the young man who gave him the plate might have stolen it and given it to him for fear of being caught. He might even be one of the gang of his Muslim adversaries who might have hatched a plot against him so that he might be accused of the theft of the plate. As he reached the temple he saw the Mahārāja and the Gosvāmijī standing at the gate. He was all the more struck with fear. How could he imagine that they were standing there to honor and not to punish him? As he bent low to salute the Mahārāja, the Mahārāja came forward and embraced him. He said with tears in his eyes: "Tāja Khān! You are blest. Madanamohana has been so kind to you." Gosvāmijī also embraced him and said: "Tāja Khān, forgive me for debarring you from visiting Madanamohana. I thought you did not deserve to visit him because you were a Muslim. Now, I know that if there is anyone in Karaulī who really deserves to visit him that is you."

As a large number of people who had gathered on the scene saw the Mahārāja and Gosvāmin embracing with love the poor peon of the court of Karaulī, they shouted with joy: "Tāja Khān kī jaya! (Victory to Tāja Khān)"

Tāja Khān stood bewildered. The whole thing was still a mystery to him. "Why this sudden outburst of affection for me?" he wondered. "How am I blest? How has Madanamohana been kind to me?" Suddenly a thought crossed his mind. With a start he asked Gosvāmijī: "Gosvāmijī, where is that servant whom you sent with the plate?"

Gosvāmijī said, pointing to Madanamohana: "He sits there on the throne. But is he now the servant? He is the master of all, the creator and controller of the universe. Blessed are you because your love made him the servant of the servant of his servant."

As Tāja Khān heard this, his body trembled like a tree struck by a storm. Tears streamed out of his eyes. His heart was pained and he looked pityingly at Madanamohana at the thought of the trouble he had taken for him.

After this Tāja Khān became so famous that it was difficult for him to live peacefully in seclusion. He left Karaulī and no one knows where he went.

The people of Karaulī still sing a song describing Madanamohana as the servant, who stole the plate for Tāja.[7]

Bhagavān as Demonstrator at Mahārāja's College, Jaipur, and Mādho Lāla Māthura

Mādho Lāla Māthura was born in 1899. He received his Bachelor of Science degree in 1920 and became demonstrator [lecturer] in the Department of Physics at Mahārāja's College, Jaipur, in 1923.

Mādho Lāla's father and grandfather were *bhaktas*. He also had a strong inclination for *bhakti* from his childhood. Since he felt especially attracted towards Bhagavān Rāma, he took initiation from Śrī Gomatī Dāsajī of Ayodhyā in Rāma-bhakti at the age of sixteen.

He worshiped the sacred images of Sītā and Rāma with great devotion. The images were not to him what they appeared to the material eye. They were the Sītā and Rāma of the spiritual Sāketa abode themselves. While worshiping them he imagined that he worshiped them in Sāketa as their female friend. When he offered food to them, he put each morsel of food into their mouths with his own hand and then placed it aside as their grace-food, which he ate himself afterwards. When he bathed or dressed them the touch of their spiritual bodies caused tremors and horripilation in his body. When he performed the ceremony of lights (*ārati*) for them he became so overwhelmed with feeling that he could not sing because his throat was choked.

His religious cultivation (*sādhana*) was of the erotic relationship (*madhura-bhāva*) and he practiced remembering (*smaraṇa*) in the eight periods.[8] Because his heart was pure he soon became accomplished in remembering. His remembering continued even while walking or doing something else. He used to be so absorbed in it that sometimes, even when he was going to the college on his bicycle, he became unaware of his surroundings. On such occasions Rāma helped him so that he might not suffer an accident. Sometimes in the college, when he supervised the students performing experiments in the laboratory, his mind got

---

[7] *Rājasthān ke Bhakt*, 434-441.

[8] This is a way of spiritual cultivation in which the practitioner meditates on the daily sports of Kṛṣṇa or Rāma as divided into the eight parts of the day, each lasting three hours. He also imagines himself to be a participant in those sports and renders service according to his feelings.

so entangled in divine sports that he remained standing with his eyes closed without any awareness of the laboratory and the students. The students knew that he had plunged into the inner world of God and did not disturb him.

Men of the world find it difficult to remove their minds from the world and turn them towards God. They try to fix their minds on God, but their minds run towards the material world because the natural tendency is to seek the world and things that are worldly. But the natural tendency of Mādho Lāla's mind was God-ward. He tried forcibly to harness and turn it towards the world to fulfill his worldly responsibilities, but it ran forcibly towards Bhagavān Rāma and his sports. It was difficult for him to remain in himself as demonstrator. He remained mostly in the service of the lotus feet of Rāma and Sītā in his accomplished body (*siddha-deha*) as their girlfriend. Therefore, it was natural that he should at times miss his duty as demonstrator in the college. It was also natural for Rāma on such occasions to come to his help, because he loves his devotees even more than his own self.

One day Mādho Lāla kept himself busy for a long time in the service of Sītā and Rāma in meditation. When the meditation was over it was too late for him to go to the college. Still, he rushed towards the college as fast as he could. He went straight to Prof. M. S. Sonāvālā, the head of the Department of Physics and said: "Sir, I am so late. Would you kindly grant me leave for today?" Sonāvālā looked at Mādho Lāla with astonishment and said: "What?"

"Sir, I am very sorry for coming so late. I want to apply for leave."

"What do you mean, Māthura? Did you not come and sign the register?"

"No, sir."

"I saw you signing. I saw you teaching the class."

Mādho Lāla was stupefied. So was Sonāvālā. Sonāvālā asked the lab-bearer to bring the attendance register. He said to Mādho Lāla, placing the register before him: "Look, is this not your signature?"

Mādho Lāla was all the more stupefied. He kept gazing at the signature. He thought someone else might have signed for him. But that could not be, because Sonāvālā said he saw him signing.

Sonāvālā called the students. He asked them: "Did Mr. Māthura give your class today?"

"Yes sir. Today's lecture was wonderful. See, here are the notes of the lecture."

Sonāvālā looked at Mādho Lāla as he extended the notes towards him. Mādho Lāla saw that the notes related to the very subject he had to teach that day. He was taken aback. But he did not take long to understand what had actually happened. His heart was filled with a deep feeling of gratitude towards someone. A strong current of religious feeling shook him. Tears began to course down his cheeks. Tremors and horripilation appeared on his body. Somehow he controlled the feeling and went to his room. Sonāvālā and the students thought that it was all due to some temporary mental affliction from which Mādho Lāla suffered at the time.

That day Mādho Lāla had been so absorbed in remembering that he had lost all consciousness of time. His Lord Śrī Rāma had performed his duty in his guise. Does the Lord go to that extent in serving his devotee? Is it not highly immoral and illegal to pretend to be someone else and sign for him? How can he do this? There is nothing that he will not do for his devotee, who has completely surrendered himself to him, depends entirely upon him, and does nothing except that which pleases him. He does not know what is good or bad, moral or immoral, in the service of a devotee to whom he is completely sold for his love.

Mādho Lāla was one such devotee, to whom the Lord was completely sold on account of his love.

Verification of the Law of Unification

We have seen what the law of unification means in practice. It means that Bhagavān regards the pleasure and pain, needs and requirements of the devotees as his own and looks after them. In this connection Kṛṣṇa's words *yoga-kṣemaṃ vahāmy aham* in the *Gītā* (9.22) need clarification:

> Kṛṣṇa himself attends to the needs of his devotees.

The words literally mean: "I myself look after the needs and welfare of my devotees." Is this the real meaning of the verse? Why should Bhagavān himself carry the burden when there are so many other agencies to do for him whatever he wants?

The question arose in the mind of a virtuous *brāhmaṇa* of Jagannātha Purī who used to read the *Gītā* with devotion. He said: "No, this cannot be." He scored out the words *vahāmy aham* with a pen and wrote *karomy aham* which means "I arrange for the fulfillment of his needs."

The *brāhmaṇa* used to live on alms. He could not go out for alms one day because of rain. He and his wife had to fast. He went out the next day when the rain stopped. Soon after, there came to his house a handsome young boy who had a wound on his forehead, from which blood was trickling down his cheeks, and who had a load of provisions on his head. He placed the load before the *paṇḍita*'s wife and said: "Paṇḍitajī has sent these provisions." The lady was enchanted by the beauty and luster of his face, but was pained to see it smeared with blood. She asked: "Who has hurt you, my child?"

"Paṇḍitajī," replied the boy.

"What? My husband? He has a kind heart. Why should he hurt a lovely child like you?"

"I tell you Mā. It was he who pierced my forehead with a dart. He alone knows why he did it."

The boy disappeared. When the *brāhmaṇa* returned, his wife narrated to him the whole story with grief and resentment. He stood there dumbfounded. But the mystery soon became clear to him. He realized that the *Gītā* was the verbal image of Śrī Kṛṣṇa and by scoring out with his pen *vahāmy aham* from it he had inflicted a wound on his forehead. Penitential tears began to flow from his eyes and he fell senseless to the ground. On regaining consciousness he began to write the words *vahāmy aham* on every inch of blank space in his copy of the *Gītā*, for he now understood that Bhagavān himself looked after the needs and welfare of his devotees and he loved to do it more than he loved anything else.[1]

This was confirmed by the fact that Bhagavān had himself brought the provisions for the *brāhmaṇa* on his head even though he was hurt and wounded by him. This is also confirmed by what he did in the case of the elephant devotee caught by the crocodile and Prahlāda. He himself ran barefooted to deliver the elephant from the mouth of the crocodile and he himself appeared from a pillar in the form of Nṛsiṃha (the man-lion form of Viṣṇu) to save Prahlāda from Hiraṇyakaśipu. Not only this, he lifted Prahlāda onto his lap and said, licking him affectionately with his tongue: "My son, excuse me for coming late."[2]

Modern history is also full of examples that bear out the truth of Śrī Bhagavān's statement that he himself looks after the needs and welfare of his devotees.

Examples

Kṛṣṇa Himself Fought a War for Rāja Jayamala Rāṭhora

Rāja Jayamala, the son of Vīramadeva and cousin of Mīrā Bāi, was born in 1507 C.E. and ascended the throne of Meḍtā in 1543. He was a great warrior. Stories of his extraordinary valor have been narrated

---

[1] H. Poddar, *The Philosophy of Love (Bhakti-sūtra of Devarṣi Nārada)*, 141-143.

[2] These are well known stories from the *Bhāgavata Purāṇa*. [Ed.]

even by Muslim historians like Abū al-Fazl ibn Mubārak, Badā ūni, and Firishtah.

Rao Māladeva, the ruler of Jodhpur, a much bigger state than Meḍtā, attacked Meḍtā twenty-two times and each time he had to face defeat at the hands of Rāja Jayamala.

Rāja Jayamala was also a great devotee like Mīrā. He regarded his Ṭhākura Śyāmasundara (Kṛṣṇa) as the actual ruler of his state and he ruled it on his behalf as his agent. Every morning he spent four hours with Śyāmasundara while worshiping him in a room in his palace. At the time he used to be so absorbed in worship that he forgot all about the world, as if he drew Śyāmasundara into the temple of his heart and closed the door from the inside. No one was allowed to enter the room at that time. No one could go and inform him even if the worst happened, even if an enemy attacked and threatened to overrun the state.

Māladeva came to know of this. In 1554 he attacked Meḍtā with a large army during the very hours in which Jayamala was engaged in worship. The army included besides Pṛthvīrāja Jetāvata, the commander-in-chief, his son Rāyamala.

As soon as the prime minister (*dīvān*) saw the enemy coming, he became restless to inform Jayamala but did not have the courage to do so. He requested the mother of the king to somehow inform him. She felt compelled by the impending disaster to inform him. She went to the room where Jayamala was engaged in worship. She said to him: "My son, the enemy has attacked. The army is impatiently waiting for your orders." The words did not reach the ears of Jayamala. He had drunk deeply of the nectar of love and all his senses were so engaged in the loving service of Śyāmasundara that no message from the outside world could reach him. The mother of the king shouted still louder, but in vain. She shook him hard with both of her hands. Then with a start he opened his eyes. His mother told him of the invasion. He said: "Let the Lord's will be done," and again went into trance.

The war-cry and sound of the war drums of the enemy could now be distinctly heard. The enemy was about to enter the city. The people were terrified and began to run helter-skelter. Just then they saw Jayamala and his seven thousand soldiers pouncing upon the enemy as hawks fall upon their prey. Jayamala on his horse darted through the lines of the enemy with such lightning speed, brandishing his sword and slaying and slashing right and left, that within a short time the field was strewn with the dead bodies of thousands of soldiers. Pṛthvīrāja Jetāvata died. Māladeva and his army fled. Rāyamala lay wounded by the sword of Jayamala on the field. Rāyamala had seen that it was not Jayamala but a blue colored boy in budding youth who wounded him and disappeared.

As soon as worship was over Jayamala went out to fight the enemy. He sent for his horse. He saw that the horse was tired and his body was sweating. He asked the horse-keeper: "Who rode the horse?"

The horse-keeper looked at him with surprise and said: "Mahārāja, who else would ride it? Did you not yourself go riding to fight the enemy?"

The next moment Jayamala saw his victorious army coming towards the palace with a crowd shouting: "Meḍtā Nareśa Jayamala Mahārāja kī jaya! (Victory to great king Jayamala, king of Meḍtā!)" He did not take long to understand that it was his beloved Śrī Kṛṣṇa who had fought the battle for him.

Immediately Jayamala went out of the city to the place where the battle was fought. He saw heaps of dead bodies lying there along with the wounded Rāyamala. Jayamala accosted him lovingly and asked him to describe how the battle was fought. Rāyamala looked at him with astonishment and asked: "Raojī, who was that dark-blue faced, young warrior in your army who rode through our army with lightning speed killing so many soldiers in the twinkling of an eye and wounding me? His beauty was as mystifying as his valor. The soldiers kept looking at him while he rode past slaying and slashing. I do not know what has happened to me after seeing him. My heart yearns to see him again."

Jayamala said with tears streaming out of his eyes: "Who can that warrior be except my Lord? Who can be so valiant as he? Who can risk his life like this for a small fry like me? You are fortunate that you saw him and were wounded by him. All your sins have been washed away by the blood you shed and your heart has become pure. That is why divine love has sprouted in your heart and you have begun to yearn to see him."

Jayamala admired Rāyamala's fate, because he had been blessed with a sight of the Lord, but cursed himself because he was not so blessed. His heart was filled with resentment against the Lord. He went to the Chārabhujā Temple in his state, stood before the image, resting against a pillar of the temple, and said: "Lord, I cannot tolerate this. You have appeared to Rāyamala, my enemy, and blessed my horse, but when my turn came you left the horse in the stable and disappeared."

Then, pointing a knife at his chest he said: "If you do not appear to me right now, I shall thrust this knife into my heart and die." The Lord saw that he was actually going to do what he said. He trembled. He could have come down from the altar and held back his hand. But a second's delay would have been dangerous. Therefore, he appeared from the very pillar against which the king was standing, held back his hand and disappeared after giving him a sight of himself.

Even today that pillar in the temple of Chārabhujā in Meḍtā is regarded as sacred and is worshiped.

Next morning, when Jayamala was worshiping Śyāmasundara, he saw that one of his earrings was missing. He searched for it in the room, but it could not be found. He thought that he might have dropped it on the field the previous day while fighting. He went to the field with some of his soldiers and began to search for it. He found it lying at a particular spot. On that spot he constructed a pond to commemorate the battle fought by the Lord on the field. The pond was called Kuṇḍala-kunda, the Pond of the Earring. It exists even now.

Girirāja Himself Brought Grace-food for Lālā Bābu

We have already referred to Lālā Bābu, the governor of Orissa, who renounced everything and became a recluse.[3] He went to Vraja, saw all the holy places associated with the sports of Kṛṣṇa and then began to live in a cave in Govardhana and perform private worship. Every morning he went on circumambulation of Girirāja (Govardhana Mountain). After circumambulation he performed private worship in the cave throughout the day. Late in the evening he went out begging for alms (*madhukārī*).

One day while he was out on circumambulation the priest of the temple of Giridhārī said: "Bābā, do not go for alms today. I shall myself go to your cave in the evening and give you the grace-food of Giridhārī."

In the evening it started raining and continued to rain till night. The rain was so torrential that it was impossible for the priest to go out. There was no end to his anxiety for Lālā Bābu, who, he thought, must be very hungry, because he ate grace-food only once after the day's circumambulation and private worship. When the rain slowed down he thought of going to Lālā Bābu with grace-food. He had already filled a plate with grace-food for him inside the temple. When he went

[3] *Saints of Vraja*, 105-121.

inside the temple, he was surprised to find the plate missing. There was no time to think how the plate could have disappeared. Quickly he arranged grace-food on another plate and proceeded towards the cave.

As soon as he reached there Lālā Bābu said: "What is this, dear priest? What more have you brought? I have not been able to eat all that you brought before. See, it is still lying there."

The priest was surprised to see the missing plate and grace-food in the cave. "Who brought it?" he asked at once.

Lālā Bābu looked with amazement at the priest and said: "What? Do you mean to say you did not bring it?"

"I neither brought it nor sent it to you through someone else."

"No, no! You brought it. I reprimanded you for coming all the way in the rain and getting drenched, but you smiled and went away. I wonder how you have forgotten everything so soon. Have you taken *bhāṅg*?"[4]

The priest knew he had not taken *bhāṅg*. He looked at Lālā Bābu for some time with tears flowing profusely from his eyes. Then suddenly reaching his hand out to touch his feet he said: "Bābā, you are fortunate. You have so won over Girirāja by your love that he could not bear to see you hungry. He himself came to you in my guise with the grace-food in the rain and did not mind getting drenched."

On hearing this Lālā Bābu's entire body was filled with the eight *sāttvika* conditions and he fell unconscious on the ground. On regaining consciousness he said with tears in his eyes: "Prabhu! You took so much trouble for this undeserving servant of yours!"

Was Lālā Bābu undeserving? He had relinquished the office of governor, renounced family and everything else, and was day and night thinking of Kṛṣṇa and no one else. It is only for devotees like him that Kṛṣṇa has said: "I take care of them."

Rādhā Brought Food for Madhusūdana Dāsa Bābājī

While still a child, Madhusūdana Dāsa Bābā heard of a boy of handsome blue color, who lived in Vṛndāvana, who was joyful and frolicsome and charmingly sweet and affectionate, who loved to play the flute, whose company was very enjoyable and on attaining whom there was nothing else that remained to be attained. His name was Kṛṣṇa.

[4] An Indian narcotic substance.

Since then Madhusūdana Dāsa Bābā always thought of Kṛṣṇa and was often lost in the thought. As he grew older he learnt more about him and became impatient to meet him. One day he sneaked out of home and went to Vṛndāvana.

In Vṛndāvana he practiced the private worship of passionate *bhakti* and became accomplished (*siddha*). He had the special favor of Rādhā. There are several stories regarding Rādhā's mercy on him, showing how she looked after him, just as Kṛṣṇa looked after the well-being of his devotees.

Once he developed a sore on his foot. It became very difficult for him to walk or move. He could not even go out for alms-begging. He decided to go to some lonely place and fast unto death. With great difficulty he went to a thick forest at night and lay there. He kept chanting the name of Rādhā. Two days passed without even a drop of water. On the third day came a Vrajavāsī girl with bread and water and said: "Bābā, why are you lying here? I am tired of searching for you. You did not come for alms yesterday and the day before that. My mother has sent alms for you." She placed the alms before him and said: "Bābā, eat."

Bābā had known the girl and her parents for a long time. He said: "Lālī, why have you come here? How did you come to know that I was here?"

"Oh! I come to know everything. Now don't waste time, eat."

"I will not eat."

"Why will you not eat? My mother has asked me to make you eat in my presence and not to return until you have eaten. The suffering of the body is an insignificant affair. It comes and goes. Why commit suicide on account of it? Now start eating."

Bābā could not disregard the sweet and loving command of the girl. He ate everything she had brought. Then he said: "Do not come again."

The girl went away. As she was going she looked again and again at Bābā with a mysterious smile. Simultaneously, Bābā felt that the suffering of his body was gone. He opened the bandage on his foot. To his surprise he found that the sore had disappeared. The whole thing aroused suspicion in his mind. He went to the house of the girl and asked her mother, "Where is Lālī?"

"Lālī has gone to her father-in-law's."

"When did she go?"

"About three months ago."

Then Bābā understood everything. He returned to his cottage without saying anything further for fear of publicity. But very soon it became known to everyone that he had been mercifully blessed by Rādhā, for the sore on his foot had suddenly disappeared and his emotional state had also undergone a sudden change. He always cried: "Hā Rādhe Karuṇamayī (O Rādhā, Embodiment of Compassion)" and wept.

Kṛṣṇa Pays Revenue for Kiśana Sinha Rāṭhora

Ṭhākura Kiśana Sinha Rāṭhora was the younger brother of Bāgha Sinha Rāṭhora, the chief of Garabadesara in the state of Bikāner. He was born in 1590 and lived with his maternal grandfather in Shekhāvatī (Udayapur). His only occupation was the mental service of Muralīdhara, Kṛṣṇa the flutist, in which he was always lost. His devotion to Kṛṣṇa increased day by day. After some time he became so restless for the sight of him that it became impossible for him to live without seeing him. He resolved to fast until he saw him. Three days and nights passed without his taking a morsel of food or a drop of water. His relations and the *paṇḍitas*, well versed in the scriptures, tried to persuade him to give up his resolve. The *paṇḍitas* said: "the scriptures say that Bhagavān is completely free. He can by no means be compelled to give a vision of himself by fasting."

He replied: "Whatever you say, I shall break my fast only when Bhagavān gives me a sight of himself. I shall either see him or die. In either case I shall be relieved of the pain of suffering in separation from him, which has become intolerable."

Kiśana Sinha's resolve was not an empty resolve. It was filled with divine love. Kṛṣṇa cannot be compelled to give a sight of himself by fasting even if one fasts unto death. But he is compelled by divine love. He became restless to give a sight of himself to Kiśana Sinha. But his ways are inscrutable. He appeared to him in the guise of an old *brāhmaṇa* and said: "My son, heed the advice of your relations. Bhagavān is not pleased by fasting. Break your fast."

Kiśana Sinha did not pay heed. He did not even look at the *brāhmaṇa.*

The *brāhmaṇa* then said: "See. I am a hundred-year-old *brāhmaṇa* who has done penance and realized *brahman.* Therefore, you take seeing me as the seeing of Bhagavān and break your fast."

Kiśana Sinha still remained heedlessly looking downwards.

At last Bhagavān had to say: "My son, I am no other than Bhagavān. I could not remain unconcerned by your condition. So I have come to give you a sight of myself. Now see me and break your fast."

Kiśana Sinha said: "If you are Bhagavān, I bow down to you. But how am I to know that you are Bhagavān?"

"Son, Bhagavān is by nature truthful. He does not tell a lie. Therefore, believe me."

"If you are really Bhagavān, excuse me for saying that what you have just said is itself a lie. I can say on the testimony of the *Bhāgavata Purāṇa* that you speak more lies than truths. The scriptures say that for you there is no difference between truth and untruth. You are by nature truthful only because your lie is also true."

Perhaps Bhagavān wanted him to say that he was a liar, because he is more pleased by the reproaches of a devotee than by his praises. He smiled approvingly and said: "Well, well. Now look upon me."

Kiśana Sinha saw Śrī Kṛṣṇa, with a peacock feather on his head, a flute in his hand and a bewitching smile on his lips, standing before him and radiating the blue luster of his body, cool and soothing like a thousand moons.[5]

Kiśana Sinha saw his Lord. With tears of love streaming out of his eyes and with tremors and horripilation affecting his entire body, he fell at his feet saying: "Prabhu, Prabhu!"

Kṛṣṇa lifted him up and said lovingly: "Now, what can I do for you? You should ask for some boon."

Kiśana Sinha said: "Prabhu, what shall I ask for? If you want to give me something, give me the boon that my *bhakti* for your feet remains firm and I may have a sight of you in your present form whenever I want it.

Kṛṣṇa said: "The boon is granted." He was, however, not satisfied with this. He said: "You now go and rule Garabadesara."

"But my brother rules there, Prabhu," said Kiśana Sinha.

"On the fourth day from today he will die fighting in a battle and you will succeed him," said Śrī Kṛṣṇa and disappeared.

As Śrī Kṛṣṇa had ordained Kiśana Sinha started for Garabadesara the same day. On the way he met the chieftains of Garabadesara who were going to Udayapur to inform him of the death of Bāgha Sinha and to take him to Garabadesara for enthronement, because Bāgha Sinha had

---

[5] *Kiśana-prakāśa*, 43.

no son.

Kiśana Sinha was enthroned. He governed the state but formally because most of his time was spent in mental service, in which he had become accomplished. This became known to everyone on account of a particular episode.

Once he was traveling on horse-back with Mahārāja Karṇa Sinha of Bikāner. On the way, at the usual time of worship, he covered himself with a piece of cloth and began his mental service. In the course of the mental service, when he was going to offer curds to the Lord, Karṇa Sinha said: "Kiśana, are you sleeping?" Kiśana Sinha was absorbed in service and was totally unaware of the external world. The words of Karṇa Sinha did not reach him. Karṇa Sinha then drew his horse nearer and pulled the cloth from over his head. He was shaken and the curds he was going to offer fell on the horse. Karṇa Sinha said: "What is this?" He kept quiet. But on Karṇa Sinha's insistence he told him everything. From that day forward Karṇa Sinha began to respect him as a saint.

Ever since Kiśana Sinha was blessed with the sight of Śrī Kṛṣṇa, Kṛṣṇa used to be with him like an invisible companion and always looked after his welfare.

Once Kiśana Sinha could not deposit the revenue he owed to the Bikāner state in time because he had spent a lot in the service of the poor and the needy. On receiving a reminder from the treasury he promised to pay the revenue by the next Dīpāvalī festival. But he forgot all about it because of being always engaged in mental service. One day when he saw his palace being decorated with lamps, he asked his servants: "Is it Dīpāvalī today?" The servants replied: "Yes, Mahārāja." He felt thunderstruck because it was the first time in his life that he proved false. Quickly, he collected the money and started for Bikāner the same evening. He reached Bikāner the next morning. When he went to the treasury to deposit the revenue, the treasury officer said: "Ṭhākura Sāhib, you were anxious to return to Garabadesara yesterday. What prevented you from going?"

"When did I come? I have just arrived here. I am sorry that I could not come to deposit the revenue by Dīpāvalī as promised."

The treasury officer looked at him with surprise and said: "What did you say? Did you not deposit the revenue yesterday?"

"I was in Garabadesara till evening yesterday."

The officer immediately sent for the accounts book. Showing it to Kiśana Sinha, he said: "See. This is the money you deposited and this is your signature, is it not?"

Kiśana Sinha looked attentively at the register and said: "The signature is exactly like mine." He stood dazed for a while, but tears soon streamed out of his eyes. He understood that it was Muralīdhara who had come and paid the revenue for him so that his promise might not prove false. Who else could have come in his exact guise and sign exactly like him? Even if someone could, why should he take so much trouble for him? But Muralīdhara took pride and felt pleasure in doing such things for his devotees. He always kept close to his devotee like his shadow and took care of him. He may forget his own self but never his devotee. He may get his work done by his partial manifestations, but when he finds his devotee in difficulty, he himself runs to help him. He may speak the truth or lie any number of times, but he takes care to see that what his devotee says does not prove to be a lie. He derives great satisfaction in converting his lie to truth.

Mahārāja Karṇa Sinha came to know of this episode. When Karṇa Sinha went to pay respect to him, he embraced him and said: "Kiśana Sinha, you are blest and I am blest on account of you, because Bhagavān came to my treasury and deposited revenue with his own hands. From today you are freed from revenue. Neither will you have to come for the payment of revenue, nor will Bhagavān."

Another sport of Muralīdhara showing how he takes care of his devotees is like this:

Kiśana Sinha had a kind heart. He was kindly disposed even towards animals. But he had often to go hunting with the Mahārāja, which he did not like. Once while hunting he pursued a pregnant deer at the instance of the Mahārāja and cut it to pieces with his sword. The fawn in the womb of the deer was also cut into two. The manner in which the deer looked towards him while dying hurt him so much that he resolved not to keep the sword with which he had killed that innocent animal anymore. But not to keep a sword would have been against his honor as a Rājapūta chieftain. Therefore, he began secretly to keep a wooden sword in his sheath. For several days no one knew about it. But once a Rājapūta chief who bore ill will against him came to know of it. He spoke to Mahārāja about it. The Mahārāja did not believe him. The chief said: "You ask him once to take his sword out of the sheath. If you do not find that it is wooden, you may chop my head off."

The Mahārāja thought Kiśana Sinha would feel insulted if he asked him to take out his sword and show whether it was made of steel or wood. One day in a meeting of the chiefs he asked them all in a light mood to unsheath their swords so that he might see whose sword shone the most. Everyone unsheathed his sword, but Kiśana Sinha sat quietly, as if he had not heard. The Mahārāja said: "Kiśana Sinha, you also show your sword."

"Mahārāja, my sword is not worth showing, because it is made of wood."

The other chiefs thought that he said that in ironical humor. The Mahārāja said: "How does it matter if it is made of wood? You must also show it."

Kiśana Sinha stood up and took the sword out of the sheath. He was surprised to see that it was made of steel and shone as bright as the sword of any other chief. He remained wondering at the mercy of Muralīdhara. But Mahārāja said to the chief who had reported against him: "You swine. You did not hesitate to slander a brave and honorable chief like Kiśana Sinha. Now get ready to have your head chopped off."

Kiśana Sinha could not remain silent. He said: "Mahārāja, the fault is not his. My sword was wooden. I am myself now surprised to see that it is made of steel. Obviously, the wood was miraculously changed into steel by Muralīdhara. Since the day I killed that innocent deer, I started keeping a wooden sword out of penitence."

The Mahārāja's anger subsided. Kiśana Sinha rose still higher in his esteem. He said: "Kiśana Sinha, now you need not also come to my court. I shall myself go and meet you when I want."

Kiśana Sinha's sword is still preserved in Garabadesara. On Dīpāvalī day people worship it, because it is the sword made by Muralīdhara.

Rādhā Restored the Eyes of the Blind Bābā of Madanaṭera

About eighty years ago there lived in Vṛndāvana in a cottage near Madanamohana's temple a blind Bābā. No one knew his name. But people called him Madanaṭeravāle Bābā (the Bābā of Madanaṭera[6]), because he lived mostly in the seclusion of Madanaṭera. Early in the morning after bathing in the Yamunā, he used to go and hide himself in the bowers of Madanaṭera. He remained there till evening. All the time he shed tears in remembrance of Rādhā and Kṛṣṇa and their sports. In the

[6]The area around the Madanamohana temple in Vṛndāvana.

evening he went to the temple of Govindajī, prayed to him and wept. After returning from there he received alms from three or four houses, ate and slept. But his tears never stopped.

It was because of weeping continuously that he lost his eyesight. He was not sorry for it, because the eyes with which he could not see Kṛṣṇa were of no use to him.

But now Bābā had been weeping for forty years. Life was about to end and the utmost limits of his patience were crossed. The pain of separation became unbearable. Sometimes on account of that he fell unconscious and remained lying on the ground amidst the trees for hours. There was no one to attend to him, no one to sympathize with him. The twittering of small birds and the calls of the cuckoos and peacocks tried to awaken him, but in vain.

When the pain of separation becomes unbearable to the *bhakta*, it also becomes unbearable to Bhagavān. Rādhā and Kṛṣṇa could no more remain in separation from Bābā. Once while taking a stroll, they came to Madanaṭera where Bābā was weeping under a tree.

Rādhā said to Kṛṣṇa: "Pyāre (beloved), Bābā is always weeping. Why not make him laugh a little?"

Kṛṣṇa went to Bābā and said: "Bābā, why are you weeping? Has someone beaten you or deprived you of something?"

"Oh no. You go away," said the blind Bābā in rage.

"Bābā, I shall bring you flat-breads or buttermilk or whatever you want. But you should not weep," again said Kṛṣṇa entreatingly.

"O cowherd, go and tend your cows. Why have you come here to trouble me?" Bābā turned his face from Kṛṣṇa as he said this.

Kṛṣṇa went back and said to Rādhā: "Bābā does not listen. He only weeps and weeps."

Rādhā said: "Pyāre, you couldn't make him laugh. See how I make him laugh."

She went to Bābā and said: "Bābā, why do you weep? Have you lost your wife?"

Bābā laughed and said: "Lālī, I never had a wife."

"I see. So you weep because you have no one whom you can regard as you own," said Rādhā in a tone of deep sympathy.

Bābā said grievously: "No, Lālī. I do not weep for that. I weep because those who are mine have forgotten me."

"Who are they, Bābā?"

"Lālī, you do not know. One of them is the heartless son of Nanda, who always tempts and tantalizes but never shows himself. And the other? Oh, what shall I say about her, Lālī? The other is Rādhā who has also become heartless in his company."

Rādhā felt grievously hurt in the tendermost corner of her heart.

"Me? Me, heartless?" she burst out. Then trying to conceal herself she said: "Bābā, my name is also Rādhā. Tell me what you want."

"What should I say, Lālī? What can I want except to see them?"

"Bābā, you are very simple. You do not know that you cannot see them even if they show themselves because you have no eyes."

"Lālī, you are simple, not I. You do not know that I will get my eyesight back as soon as they touch my eyes with their lotus hands."

Rādhā could not restrain herself anymore. She touched one eye of Bābā with her lotus hand. Kṛṣṇa touched the other. Immediately Bābā's eyesight was restored. He saw both Rādhā and Kṛṣṇa, the twin divinities of his heart, standing before him in all their resplendent beauty and looking at him lovingly and mercifully.

What an example of looking after needs (*yoga-kṣemaṃ vahāmy aham*). Rādhā and Kṛṣṇa opened not only his physical eyes but also his spiritual eyes by a single act of mercy.

Lord Jagannātha Lied to Save Jagadbandhu Mahāpātra

During the reign of Mahārāja Pratāparudra, Jagadbandhu Mahāpātra was one of the priests in the temple of Lord Jagannātha in Purī.[7] He was the most learned, the most devoted, and the most respected of all the priests in Purī. He served Jagannātha with all his heart and soul from morning till evening. Jagannātha was his beloved, his guru, his life and his soul. Jagannātha was the only one whom he loved and loved so dearly. He knew no one else except him.

One day suddenly the sky of Purī resounded with the sound of hundreds of conch shells, drums, *mṛdaṅga, turī, bherī* and other instruments. A number of voices announced the coming of the Mahārāja to the temple. Jagadbandhu Mahāpātra was so absorbed in the service of Jagannātha that he was unaware of everything else. The attendants of the temple came running and said to him: "Mahāpātra, Mahāpātra! Mahārāja is coming. See. He is already at the gate."

---

[7] Atulakṛṣṇa Gosvāmin, *Bhakter Jaya*, vol. II, 22-34.

Mahāpātra was startled to see the Mahārāja. Hastily he stepped up to see if there were any flowers on the head of Jagannātha. He was appalled to see that not a single flower was there. It was incumbent on him to offer grace-flowers, flowers already offered to Jagannātha, to the Mahārāja as the blessing of Jagannātha. He did not know what to do. There was no time to get flowers from elsewhere, no time also for reflecting. He put Jagannātha's grace flowers from his own head back on the head of Jagannātha. The very next moment the Mahārāja arrived. He extended his hands towards Mahāpātra for grace-flowers. Mahāpātra picked the flowers from the head of Jagannātha and gave them to him. The Mahārāja touched them with his eyes and went.

In the evening while sitting on his throne the Mahārāja sometimes touched the flowers with his forehead, sometimes with his eyes and sometimes with his nose to smell them. In the process he happened to see some black hairs in the flowers. "What is this?" he said with a start. "How could there be hairs in the flowers on the head of Jagannātha? Mahāpātra must have put the flowers from his own head on the head of Jagannātha and given them to me as the grace of Jagannātha." Immediately he called some attendants and said: "Go and bring Mahāpātra at once."

The attendants went and brought him. In a harsh tone the Mahārāja said to him: "Mahāpātra. When did hairs grow on the Lord's head? See. There are hairs in the grace-flowers you gave me. Tell me frankly where the hairs came from, otherwise face death."

Mahāpātra stood still, as if life had already gone out of him. He remembered Jagannātha and said: "Prabhu, save me. I do not fear death. I am afraid that your name will be disgraced if your servant is punished. Just now I cannot escape death without lying. So let me for the time being save myself by telling a lie. Afterwards you may do what you like."

After Mahāpātra had thus prayed to Jagannātha, he said to the Mahārāja laughingly: "Mahārāja, don't you know that Jagannātha has hair on his head?"

"What do you say Mahāpātra? Hairs on the head of the wooden image of Jagannātha? Have you gone mad? How long can you save yourself by telling this lie?"

"Mahārāja, you can go and see for yourself. If you find that I am telling a lie, you give me whatever punishment you like."

Mahāpātra did not go home. He went straight to the temple and stood before Jagannātha. He said with folded hands and tears flowing from his eyes. "Omniscient Prabhu, you know that I have not come to you to pray for my life. Capital punishment I certainly deserve, because I have committed a grave offense by offering to you the grace-flowers I had on my head. For this if you cut my head off with your discus, I will not be sorry. But kindly prevent me from punishment at the hands of the Rāja. Counting on your mercy I have spoken a lie to him. You are known to have forgiven your servants and honored them even after being offended or insulted by them. The footprint of Bhṛgu Ṛṣi on your chest is proof of this. You must do something to save me from the hands of the Rāja tonight. If you don't, I shall have to die at his hands tomorrow. In that case, I shall take poison and commit suicide before dawn."

Mahāpātra collected some poison and went home after thus praying to the Lord. At home he did not eat anything but meditated on Jagannātha and weeping and sobbing finally offered at the Lord's lotus feet his life and soul and everything else and slept.

Lord Jagannātha appeared to him in a dream and said: "Mahāpātra, you are dear to me. You have no reason to worry or be despondent. What can the Mahārāja do to you? You are worried about the lie you have spoken to him. Do you think what you said to him was a lie? Am I bald? You can see in the morning that black and thick, curly hair adorns my head."

Mahāpātra's sleep broke. It was about 3:00 a.m. Silence and darkness prevailed all round. But his heart was lit with a new ray of light. He was confident that the Lord had granted his prayer and his lie had been corrected. He was anxious to go to the temple and see with his own eyes the curly hair on the Lord's head. He got up from bed, took a bath, rushed to the temple with joy. Tears were streaming out of his eyes, hairs standing on end, and his body trembling. He saw that the head of Jagannātha was covered with hair, black and bright like the black bee and beautifully decorated with flowers.

Mahāpātra started serving Jagannātha delightedly with a feeling of deep gratitude towards him. As soon as the day dawned the Mahārāja arrived. He said to Mahāpātra: "Now show me the hair on Jagannātha's head."

"Mahārāja, you can come near and see yourself."

The Mahārāja went near the altar. He saw the hair but could not believe it. He said: "Mahāpātra, you are a rogue. You can tell a lie and to cover it up you toy with Jagannātha to such an extent. Have you not planted artificial hair on his head with melted wax? Tell me!"

"Mahārāja, what can I say? You can examine whether the hairs are artificial or natural."

The Mahārāja angrily pulled out some hairs from the head of Jagannātha. As he did this he was shocked to see drops of blood appearing on the Lord's head and fell unconscious on the ground. On regaining consciousness he fell at the feet of Mahāpātra and said with eyes swimming in tears and throat choked with emotion: "Mahāpātra, forgive me. I did not know that Jagannātha is so kind to you, that he is so subjugated by your love. I did not know that *bhakta* and Bhagavān are but one, that the pain and pleasure, comfort and discomfort, fortune and misfortune, honor and dishonor of the *bhakta* touch the heart of Bhagavān as much as they touch the heart of the *bhakta* and there is nothing that he will not do to save him from disaster or disrepute. I have committed a grave offense at the feet of both Bhagavān and the *bhakta* by pulling out the hair of Bhagavān and disbelieving the *bhakta*. I am doomed. You tell me what I should do. My fate is in your hands."

With this the Mahārāja fell at the feet of Mahāpātra. Mahāpātra lifted him onto his lap and said: "Mahārāja, why grieve in vain? The fault is not yours but mine. It is I who committed the offense by offering the flowers from my own head to Jagannātha and by telling you a lie. The hairs you found in the flowers were the hairs of my head. Till yesterday there was not a single hair on the head of Jagannātha. But the merciful Lord took mercy on me and performed this sport to save my life and my honor. You should kindly forgive me."

At this time the bell rang for the ceremony of greeting (*ārati*). As both of them turned their eyes towards Jagannātha, they were stupefied to see that there was not a single hair on the head of Jagannātha.

The Mahārāja said: "Mahāpātra, what do I see now? Is this an illusion or was what we saw before an illusion?"

Mahāpātra said: "Mahārāja, neither is this an illusion nor is what we saw before. Both are the sport of Jagannātha and both are true."

It is obvious that Jagannātha performed this sport only to convert his devotee's lie into truth. The question, however, arises: what was the necessity of this sport? Could the Lord not take simpler steps to protect Mahāpātra and to avoid unnecessary agitation in the mind of the Mahārāja? Could he not ask the Mahārāja directly or in a dream to forgive Mahāpātra? Could he not by his inconceivable power prevent the Mahārāja from seeing the hairs on the flowers? Could he not turn the hairs themselves into flowers? Should he who is regarded as the protector of *dharma* or righteousness have done the unrighteous act of converting a lie into truth?

A possible answer to the questions is that the Lord has infinite forms and the inconceivable power of holding together even forms that contradict each other. He manifests himself in a particular form to suit a particular occasion. Mahāpātra did not actually speak a lie, because his form with curly hair on his head is also one of the infinite forms he has. Jagannātha only confirmed what he said by manifesting that form.

This answer may be correct, but it would not please Jagannātha, because it is based on his godly might (*aiśvarya*). There is another answer which is according to his essential nature as *rasa*. The answer is that even though the Lord is himself the truth and the protector of truth and righteousness, there is nothing unrighteous or immoral that he cannot do for the sake of his devotee. It is known that he stole rice-pudding (*khīra*) for Mādhavendra Purī. Could he not, therefore, support a lie or convert a lie into truth for the sake of Mahāpātra? It is true that he could ask the priest to go and give rice-pudding to Mādhavendra Purī. He could also ask the Mahārāja to forgive Mahāpātra. But could he thereby prove his subjugation by the devotee as much as he did by stealing the pudding or supporting the lie? He relishes not only being completely subjugated by his devotees, but also showing that he is so subjugated by them.

Lord Jagannātha Rendered Menial Service to Mādhava Dāsa Bābā

Mādhava Dāsa Bābā was a disciple of Īśvara Purī (15-16th centuries) and a guru-brother of Śrī Caitanya Mahāprabhu.[8] He was the biggest *paṇḍita* of Jagannātha Purī. The fame of his learning had spread all over the country. He used his learning in the study of the scriptures and the pursuit of *bhakti*. He was a devotee of Jagannātha. His devotion

[8]Harirāma Vyāsa, *Nava-ratna*, 1.8. He is referred to only as Mādhava in this text and is given as the guru of Harirāma Vyāsa. There is no mention of his being a *bābā* there. The use of the word *baba* here seems to be anachronistic since that institution did not develop until later, perhaps as late as the 18th or early 19th centuries, in Caitanya Vaiṣṇavism. This account of his life comes from the *Bhakta Māla* of Nābhā Dāsa. It is biography 89 in Lāla Dāsa's Bengali translation of Nābhā Dāsa's text. [Ed.]

to Jagannātha increased to such an extent that he forgot all about the world and his own self. When the devotee forgets everything except the Lord, the Lord assumes the responsibility of looking after his needs and welfare. The life of Mādhava Dāsa is a series of examples of the manner and the extent to which the Lord will go in giving his protection and unstinted personal service to his devotee.

A sweeping wave of deep religious emotion (*bhāva-bhakti*) once carried Mādhava Dāsa away from the world. He went and lay on the seashore totally unaware of the world, unaware of his body and remembering only the lotus feet of Jagannātha. Three days passed without eating foot or drinking water. Jagannātha could not remain unconcerned. He said to Lakṣmī: "My devotee Mādhava Dāsa has been sitting on the sea shore without even a morsel of food for three days. Arrange to send some food for him." Lakṣmī Devī could have arranged to send food through someone, but she thought she must go and see the devotee for whom Jagannātha felt so concerned. She arranged Jagannātha's grace-food of different kinds on the golden plate of Jagannātha and took it herself to Mādhava Dāsa. She saw him sitting in deep meditation, totally unaware of the world. She did not think it proper to disturb him. She left the plate before him, looked at him closely, and returned.

When the meditation was over, Mādhava Dāsa opened his eyes. He was surprised to see the plate and the grace-food sitting before him. He understood that the grace-food was sent by Lord Jagannātha. Who else would know that he was sitting in that secluded place and had been without food for three days? Even if someone knew about it why would he take the trouble of bringing food for him on a golden plate and leave the plate there?

He ate the grace-food of Jagannātha with relish. After eating he put the plate aside and again went into meditation.

Next morning when the priest opened the altar-room, he found the plate missing. The priests of the temple went out in search of the plate and found it lying near Mādhava Dāsa. The news went around that Mādhava Dāsa had stolen the sacred image's plate. The priests tied him with ropes and lashed him. But the benign Lord took the lashes upon himself. Not a single stroke touched the body of Mādhava Dāsa. At night in a dream, Jagannātha showed his back to the priest and said: "Look. You have not beaten Mādhava Dāsa but me. You can see the signs of lashes on my back. I have myself sent the plate to him through Lakṣmī. He has not stolen it. You go and apologize to him." There was no end to the fear and penitence of the priests. They went to Mādhava Dāsa, untied him and requested him with folded hands to forgive them.

Mādhava Dāsa readily forgave them. But when the priest told him about the dream he felt excruciatingly pained at heart. He could have borne the pain of lashes on his back, but how could he bear the pain of lashes suffered by the Lord for his sake? He fell on the ground like one struck with death. But the pain he suffered was different from ordinary pain, because it was mixed with the experience of the Lord's grace upon him. It was due to a stroke of grace which his tender heart could not bear.

When the strokes of the Lord's grace on the devotee begin they never end. Once Mādhava Dāsa went to the temple for a viewing of Jagannātha. While seeing Jagannātha he lost consciousness and remained standing like a statue for hours. This often happened with him and the priest knew it. He used to shake him and bring him back to consciousness so that he could leave before the temple was closed. But that day he forgot to do so. The door was closed while Mādhava Dāsa was inside. On regaining consciousness he realized that he was locked in the temple. He did not mind. He lay down in a corner and went to sleep. Since the night was cold he began to shiver. Jagannātha was moved to see his devotee shivering in sleep. He came down from the altar with his quilt, covered Mādhava Dāsa with it and went back. When Mādhava's sleep broke he saw that he was sleeping soundly, covered with a quilt, while Jagannātha was shivering with cold. This was another stroke of mercy which he could not bear.

Yet another stroke. This time the stroke was so severe that it crossed all limits of tolerance. Mādhava Dāsa suffered from acute diarrhea. He had loose motions at short intervals. So he went and lay down on the seashore. Every time he had a motion he saw Lord Jagannātha standing before him with a bowl of water for washing. Not only this. Jagannātha cleaned up the feces with his own hand. Mādhava Dāsa protested, but he did not listen. How could Mādhava Dāsa tolerate seeing him rendering this abhorrent and nauseous service with his own hands? He wished that he might die so that the Lord might not have to do that. He said to him: "Lord, you have only to wish to cure my disease. Why take all this trouble?"

The Lord said: "Mādhava, I can certainly cure you. But I don't because the fruit of actions done in the past must be enjoyed or suffered. This rule has been made by me. How can I break my own rules? If I cure your disease now, you will have to take another birth to suffer it."

"If that is so, you could ask someone else to serve me instead of serving me yourself."

"I could, if I regarded anyone else as competent for the service of my devotees. But there is one more reason why I do not do that. I do not want people to get an opportunity to laugh at me and my devotees and say: "This is the end of *bhakti.* This is how Bhagavān lets his devotee suffer."

Thus at last the Lord came out with the truth. What he said in the beginning was only a pretext. It went against his own saying to Arjuna:

> *sarva-dharmān parityajya mām ekaṃ śraraṇaṃ vraja*
> *ahaṃ tvāṃ sarva-pāpebhyo mokṣayiṣyāmi māśucaḥ*[9]
>
> Give up all other duties and surrender completely to me. I shall absolve you of all your sins. Do not worry.

It also went against his saying to Uddhava:

> *yathāgniḥ susamṛddhārciḥ karoty edhāṃsi bhasmasāt*
> *tathā mad-viṣayā bhaktir uddhavaināṃsi kṛtsnaśaḥ*[10]
>
> Just as a blazing fire reduces wood into ashes, my *bhakti* completely destroys all sins.

The rule is all right. According to the rule the fruit of all actions has to be enjoyed or suffered. But by whom? By the knowers (*jñānins*) and the workers (*karmins*), not by the *bhaktas.* For the *bhaktas* there is no rule which the Lord does not break. If he did not do so, his own declarations that he loves his *bhaktas* more than his own self and is always under their subjugation would have no meaning. He found the disease of Mādhava Dāsa an opportunity to prove the validity of his declarations. The touch of his hand cured the disease of Mādhava Dāsa.

Once a world-conquering scholar came to Purī. He challenged the scholars of Purī to a debate on scripture. Coming to know that Mādhava Dāsa was the best scholar of Purī, he went to him and said: "You will have to debate scripture with me." Mādhava Dāsa could have defeated

---

[9] *Bhagavad-gītā*, 18.66.

[10] *Bhāg.*, 11.14.19.

him in a debate on scripture, but he acknowledged defeat without entering into a debate and signed his certificate of victory in which he said clearly: "You win; I lose." The scholar went to Vārāṇasī and began to beat the drum of his victory over Mādhava Dāsa. He showed the certificate of victory to the scholars of Vārāṇasī. The scholars saw that the certificate was a certificate of the scholar's defeat rather than his victory. What was clearly written on it was: "I win; you lose." They laughed at the scholar's pride and arrogance and thought that he had gone mad. The scholar himself was amazed and angry. He thought that Mādhava Dāsa was a bit of a magician and had tricked him by magic to save his honor. He did not know that the trickster was Jagannātha who could not countenance the defeat of his devotee and loved to enhance his honor as much as the devotee shunned it.

The scholar again went to Purī and challenged him to a debate. Mādhava Dāsa again wrote: "You win; I lose." But the scholar was not satisfied. He said: "You tricked me last time. On account of you I had to suffer much humiliation in Vārāṇasī. To amend the same you must go around the city sitting on a donkey with a garland of shoes around your neck, so that the world will know that you were defeated by me. If you don't do that you must actually debate scripture with me on condition that the defeated person will ride a donkey."

Mādhava Dāsa was compelled to accept the challenge because he did not want his name to go down as that of a magician and trickster. What had magic and trickery to do with *bhakti*? But he said: "Please wait a little. Let me first go and have a bath in the sea."

He went and when he returned after the bath he was surprised to see the conquering scholar being taken around the city on the back of a donkey and a crowd of citizens following him with shouts of "Mādhava Dāsa kī Jaya! Mādhava Dāsa kī Jaya! (Victory to Mādhava Dāsa)." The citizens were surprised to see Mādhava Dāsa returning from the sea, when he had already defeated the scholar in debate on scripture and returned to his hut. They did not take long to understand that Jagannātha had gone to debate with the scholar in his place and had defeated him. They began to shout "Jaya Jagannātha" along with "Jaya Mādhava Dāsa."[11]

---

[11] Nābhā Dāsa, *Bhakta-māla*, 70.

Rādhā and Kṛṣṇa Massaged Mā Maṇi

Mā Maṇi was born with strong subconscious inclinations (*saṃskāras*) for *bhakti* which were further strengthened on account of her association with her devout grandmother with whom she lived in her childhood in the village of Galasi in the district of Burdwan, West Bengal. She used to go with her to attend readings of the *Bhāgavata* and religious discourses whenever and wherever she went.

She was married at an early age. At the age of thirty she took initiation from Śrī Jagadbandhu Maitra. Jagadbandhu was a disciple of Śrī Vijayakṛṣṇa Gosvāmin, a descendant of Śrī Advaitācārya and an accomplished saint of repute.

She passed through great vicissitudes in life, but her religious cultivation continued. In 1949 she went to Vṛndāvana and began to live in a room in Dhīra-samīra near the bank of the Yamunā. She had now passed thirty-six years of strict religious discipline and her heart was purified. On her arrival in Vṛndāvana her spiritual eye opened and she began to have visions of the sports of Kṛṣṇa. Everyday, when she sat down for meditation, she first had a vision of Śrī Vijayakṛṣṇa Gosvāmin and his wife Mā Ṭhākurāṇī Yogamāyā Devī, and then of the Vṛndāvana sports. About her experiences in Vṛndāvana she has written:

> While living in Vṛndāvana I did not go anywhere. I sat down for meditation from 3:00 or 4:00 a.m. to 8:00 or 9:00 a.m. and from 4:00 p.m. to 8:00 or 9:00 p.m. At that time Gosvāmījī (Vijayakṛṣṇa Gosvāmin) made me see the sports of Kṛṣṇa and gave necessary instructions. He asked me to record the sports as well as his instructions, which I did. Part of what I recorded has been published. The vision of the sports has been published in the book named *Śrī Śrī Vṛndāvana-līlā* and Gosvāmījī's instructions in *Śrī Śrī Upadeśāmṛta.*
>
> I had never imagined that these would be published in the form of books. But Gosvāmījī insisted on their publication. I did not want to publish them, because I did not have those experiences by dint of any qualification of my own, but by the grace of Gosvāmījī alone. Besides, I thought if people did not believe them I shall feel very much hurt at heart.
>
> But Gosvāmījī said: "In the present age there has been a

> mushroom growth of pseudo religions. People have forgotten the pure religion of Mahāprabhu. Instead of following him they are doing the very things which he forbade. Many people have lost faith in God altogether. The publication of these books will be helpful in rebuilding the proper atmosphere for Mahāprabhu's pure religion of love."[12]

We shall quote here from her *Śrī Śrī Vṛndāvana-līlā* some of the experiences recorded by her, which show how closely Kṛṣṇa and Rādhā looked after her welfare and how affectionately they were disposed towards her:

> **āśvin 11, 1949**
>
> Today in the evening I went for viewing in the temples. After I had been to three temples I went to the temple of Lālā Bābu and had a viewing of Ṭhākura Śrī Kṛṣṇa Candramā. When I was looking at Śrī Kṛṣṇa Candramā the holy name began to repeat itself in my heart and in every pore of my body with such speed that I could not control myself.[13] I felt like sitting down. But it was getting dark. If I sat down, I did not know when I would be able to get up and go home. I could also not ask anyone to help me, because I could not talk to anyone about my feeling. I only prayed in my mind to the Lord that I should somehow reach home. I started and staggering and tottering somehow reached the temple of Gopeśvara Mahādeva. I saw Gopeśvara dancing as a girlfriend (*sakhī*). I was so enchanted by that dance that I practically lost all outward consciousness. Just then a boy about seven or eight years old came and held my left hand. In the state of deep feeling I asked him: "You are going with me. How will you return alone?" He pointed to a girl of his age who was standing there. The girl came and held my right hand. Both slowly brought me home. Then I asked them: "How will you go home?" The girl pointed to Lālā Bābu standing at some distance.[14] While still in a state of deep feeling I

[12]Mā Maṇi, *Jīvana-grantha*, 39-44.

[13]With her, repetition of the holy name had become automatic.

[14]Lālā Bābu built the temple of Śrī Kṛṣṇa Candramā in Brahma-kuṇḍa in Vṛndāvana. His biography is included in *The Saints of Vraja*.

sat down on my seat. Then I saw the boy and the girl standing before me as Kṛṣṇa Candramā and Rādhārāṇī and Lālā Bābu standing before them with folded hands. I also saw Gosvāmījī there. I asked him: "Prabhu, what do I see?" He replied: "See, see to your full satisfaction. Direct perception is a matter of great fortune."[15]

Kārtik 1, 1949

I had a headache in the morning. I sat down on my seat for meditation. I saw Gosvāmījī and Mātā Ṭhākurāṇī sitting before me. Soon came a boy and a girl, both of tender age and charmingly beautiful. I said: "Who are you?"

The girl replied: "You forgot us. Didn't we come to you that day? I am Rādhā."

The boy said: "I am Kṛṣṇa."

"Are you the Kṛṣṇa and Rādhā of Vṛndāvana or are your names just Kṛṣṇa and Rādhā?"

Both laughed heartily. The laughter was so soothing to my heart. Then the girl said in a sweet voice: "We are both the Kṛṣṇa and Rādhā of Vṛndāvana. You are our own. We love you immensely. We have come because you have a headache. We shall massage a little and the headache will disappear."

"So you will serve me—you, who are so young!"

The girl said: "Who else will serve you if we don't? Who else is yours?"

"Alright, then you can massage."

Oh how sweet the touch! The headache disappeared as soon as they touched my forehead. They also disappeared.

I said to Gosvāmījī: "The last time I came to Vṛndāvana, I thought I was blest to have the kind of visitation I had by your grace. But the kind of visitation you are blessing me with this time is beyond man's imagination. It makes me feel as if I am always swimming in an ocean of bliss, peace and tranquility, that beggars all description."

---

[15] Mā Maṇi, *Vṛndāvana-līlā*, 26.

Gosvāmījī said: "The visitation you had last time is also rare. People do not have that kind of visitation. How can they have? They come to Vṛndāvana with the object of seeking the fulfillment of their desires. It is only when one surrenders to the guru, excludes from his mind all desires and always chants the holy names that a visitation is possible."[16]

Kārtik 2, 1949

Morning—I sat on my seat and started repeating the holy names. The same boy and girl came and sat down on my lap. I said: "You have come at this time?" The girl said: "We are ourselves the names you repeat. When you repeat the names, we feel attracted and come."

Evening—I sat on my seat for meditation. The holy names began to repeat themselves with lightning speed. I tried to control it but couldn't. Soon I was lost in it. Then I saw Kṛṣṇa sitting in a boat at the bank of the Yamunā. Shortly thereafter came Rādhārāṇī and her girlfriends. Kṛṣṇa took me along with them on a boating excursion. It was a long time before we came back.[17]

Kārtik 3, 1949

Morning—I was meditating. The same boy and girl came and sat on my lap. I said: "How loving and affectionate you both are! I am sorry I will not be able to see you when I go back to Purī." Both threw their arms affectionately around my neck and said: "Can we ever leave you? We shall go wherever you are as soon as you start repeating our names."

Oh how my heart began to swim in the bottomless sea of ecstatic joy to hear this![18]

---

[16]Mā Maṇi, *Śrī Śrī Vṛndāvana-līlā*, 45-6.
[17]ibid., 47-8.
[18]ibid., 48.

The Author

Dr. O.B.L. Kapoor was born in 1909. He received his Master's Degree in philosophy from the University of Allahabad in 1931 and his Doctor of Philosophy from the same unversity in 1938. He worked as a research fellow at the Indian Institute of Philosophy in Amalner, a D. Litt. scholar at the University of Allahabad, and Professor and Head of the Department of Philosophy at B. R. College, Agra, until 1952. After that he joined the Uttar Pradesh Educational Service, Class 1, and worked as Professor and Head of the Department of Philosophy, K.N. Government College, Gyanpur (Varanasi), and Principal, Government College, Gyanpur/Rampur, until his retirement in 1967.

After retirement Dr. Kapoor settled in Vrindavan, writing books and articles on religious topics related to *bhakti*. He wrote more than 30 books in Hindi and English and a large number of articles published in various journals. His writings have been acclaimed by scholars and devotees alike. He passed away in 2001 at the ashram of his guru, Śrī Gaurāṅga Dās Bābājī, in Ramanreti, Vrindavan.

Other Books by Golden Avatar Press

1. *The Prayer Project* by Paramahansa Jagadish Dass (2014, ISBN: 978-1-936135-50-9)

Coming soon:

1. *Gosvāmins of Vṛndāvana* by Dr. O.B.L. Kapoor. Edited, introduced, and annotated by Neal Delmonico.
2. *Lord Gaurāṅga, or Salvation for All* by Shishir Kumar Ghosh. Edited, introduced, and annotated by Neal Delmonico. 2 vols.

And From Blazing Sapphire Press:

1. *On Associating with Great Ones* by Śrī Kānupriya Gosvāmī. Introduced, translated, and annotated by Neal Delmonico. This volume contains some of Kānupriya Gosvāmī's lectures, translated into English for the first time, on the topic of the uplifting power of associating, that is to say, meeting and conversing with *sādhus*, the holy men and women of the tradition. This is a topic that is of fundamental importance to 20th century Caitanya Vaiṣṇava theology. The lectures were originally collected, edited, and published in Bengali as *Mahat-saṅga Prasaṅga* by Kānupriya Gosvāmī's nephew, Gauraray Das Goswami. (2014, ISBN: 978-0-9817902-9-9)

2. *Fundamentals of Vedānta*, Part 1: *The Vedānta-sāra* of Sadānanda Yogīndra and the *Prameya-ratnāvalī* of Baladeva Vidyābhūṣaṇa (trans. by Neal Delmonico). *Fundamentals of Vedānta*, Part One, is a translation, with a detailed introduction and notes, of two short Sanskrit texts, the *Vedānta-sāra* (Essence of Vedānta) of Sadānanda and the *Prameya-ratnāvalī* (Necklace of Truth-Jewels) of Baladeva, from opposite ends of the Vedāntic spectrum. Each has been used in India for centuries to introduce beginning students to the fundamental ideas of Vedānta. (2006, ISBN: 978-0-9747968-3-3)

3. *The Life and Teachings of Krishna Das Baba of Radhakund* by Zakrent Christian. This is a work on the life and teachings of a 20th century saint from the Caitanya Vaiṣṇava tradition. Krishna Das Baba was a well known practitioner and guide who lived in a community of renunciants nestled around a holy lake in North India called Radhakund (the Pond of Śrī Rādhā). His story is typical of many stories of modern Indian men and women who gave up participation in modern society to pursue religious and spiritual goals. It thus presents insight into the yearnings of many modern Indians who when faced with the challenges of modernity haved turned towards tradition. (2nd ed. 2012, ISBN: 978-0-9747968-5-7)

4. *Nectar of the Holy Name* by Manindranath Guha (trans. Neal Delmonico). This is a translation of Manindranath Guha's classic Bengali book (*Hari-nāmāmṛta-sindhu-bindu*) on the beliefs and practices centering around the "holy names" (the names of Kṛṣṇa and of his consort Rādhā) of the Caitanya Vaiṣṇava tradition. Guha's book is a good introduction to an area of theological reflection in Caitanya Vaiṣṇavism called the "theology of the holy name." (2005, ISBN: 978-0-9747968-1-9 soft; 978-0-9747968-2-6 hard)

5. *Sādhu Sādhu: a Life of Baba Śrī Tinkudi Gosvami* by Binode Bihari Dasa Babaji. This is an English translation of Śrī Binode Bihari Das Babaji's short Bengali work on the life of Baba Tinkudi Goswami, one of the great Vaiṣṇava practitioners and saints of the 20th century. This work is translated by Neal Delmonico with an introduction and annotations. It also contains two Bengali songs by his disciples remembering Tinkudi Goswami's life and some short recollections of him by some of his American disciples. (2008,

ISBN: 978-0-9747968-8-8)

6. *The Song Divine, or Bhagavad-gītā: a Metrical Rendering (with Annotations)* (English and Sanskrit edition), trans. by C.C. Caleb. This is a new edition of the delightful English metrical translation by C.C. Caleb of the Hindu classic, the *Bhagavad-gītā*, with an introduction, annotations, and an appendix. The original Sanskrit text, in both Devanāgarī and transliteration, of the *Gītā* has been included on the left hand pages for easy access and comparison with the translation. An appendix has been added containing short summaries of the teachings of the *Gītā* by many of the great commentators on the text: Śaṅkara, Yamunā Muni, Rāmānuja, Madhusūdana Sarasvatī, Viśvanātha Cakravartin, and Baladeva Vidyābhūṣaṇa. (2011, ISBN: 978-0-9817902-3-7)

7. *The Song Divine, or Bhagavad-Gita: A Metrical Rendering (with Annotations) (English-only Edition)* trans. by C.C. Caleb. This is an edition of the metrical English translation by C.C. Caleb of the great Hindu classic, the *Bhagavad-gītā*, or The Song Divine. It includes an introduction to the text, annotations drawn from the commentary of Śaṅkara, and an appendix containing some of the traditional summaries of the text from different schools of interpretation. This edition does not include the original Sanskrit text of the *Gītā*. (2012, ISBN: 978-0-9817902-8-2)

8. *Śrī Kṛṣṇa the Lord of Love*, Premananda Bharati. Premananda Bharati's classic work, *Sri Krishna: the Lord of Love*, was originally published in 1904 in New York. It is the first full-length work presenting theistic Hindu practices and beliefs before a Western audience by a practicing Hindu "missionary." Premananda Bharati or Baba (Father) Bharati had come to the USA as a result of the encouragement of his co-religionists in India and of a vision he received while living in a pilgrimage site sacred to his tradition. He arrived in the USA in 1902 and stayed until 1911 with one return journey to India in 1907 with several of his American disciples. His book was read and admired by numerous American and British men and women of the early 20th century and captured the attention of the great Russian writer Leo Tolstoy through whom Mahatma Gandhi discovered it. This new edition contains two introductions, one by Gerald T. Carney, PhD, a specialist on Premananda Bharati's

life and work and another by Neal Delmonico, PhD, a specialist on Caitanya Vaiṣṇavism, the religious tradition to which Baba Bharati belonged. In addition, the text has been edited, corrected, annotated, and newly typeset. Appendices have been added containing supporting texts and additional materials bearing on Baba Bharati's sources for some of the ideas in his book and on his life and practices in India before his arrival in the USA. (2007, ISBN: 978-0-9747968-7-1)

9. *Śrīmad-Bhagavad-Gītā (Sanskrit Edition)* ed. and introduced by Neal Delmonico. This is an edition of the *Bhagavad-gītā* in the original language of the text, Sanskrit. No translation of the text is given in this book. Only a Roman transliteration is provided alongside the Devanāgarī version and a number of the most common variant readings in footnotes. There are hundreds of translations of the *Gītā* in various of the languages of the world and some of them include the text in either its native script, which is called Devanāgarī (the city of the gods), or in some transliterated format. A few even include word-by-word translations. But, many translations include neither text nor word equivalences. This edition is for those who would like to have access to and get to know the text itself better. It can be paired with any of the translations available in any language, including our own companion volume called the *The Song Divine*, which is a reprint/re-edition of the old classic verse translation of C. C. Caleb completed in India in 1911. (2012, ISBN: 079-1-936135-00-4)

10. *Vaishnava Temple Music in Vrindaban: the Radhavallabha Songbook* by Guy L. Beck. This is a collection of 108 songs from the Radhavallabha tradition, a major North Indian *bhakti* tradition dating from the 16th century. The songs have been collected by ethnomusicologist Guy L Beck over a period of thirty years during which time he paid many visits to the religious headquarters of the sect, in Vrindaban, UP, India. In the book, Beck analyzes each song, discussing its rhythmic characteristics and its melodic structure within the raga system of classical Indian music. The verbal text for each song is given along with a faithful translation into English. In a long introduction, Beck discusses the development of religious music in India with reference to the special history and contributions of the Radhavallabha tradition. Two CDs filled with

recordings of sample music are available free to purchasers of the book and the entire collection of recordings covering 18 expertly mastered CDs is available for purchase separately. (2011, ISBN: 978-0-9817902-4-4)

Coming soon from Blazing Sapphire:

1. *The Blazing Sapphire (Ujjvala-nīlamaṇi)* by Rūpa Gosvāmin (translation by Neal Delmonico). In three volumes. In Sanskrit and English with introduction, notes, and the commentary of Śrī Jīva Gosvāmin.

2. *My Gurudeva: a short biography of Siddha Manohara Dāsa Bābājī* by Navadvīpa Dāsa with excerpts from the original works of Siddha Bābā. Translation, introduction, and annotation by Neal Delmonico.

3. *In Praise of Śrī Kṛṣṇa's Sports (Śrī Kṛṣṇa-līlā-stava)*, the first theological/meditational text of the Caitanya Vaiṣṇava tradition, by Sanātana Gosvāmī. Translation, introduction, and annotation by Neal Delmonico.

4. *Sacred Rapture: a Study of the Religious Aesthetic of Śrī Rūpa Gosvāmin* by Neal Delmonico.

5. *The Eight Instructions of Śrī Caitanya (Śrī Caitanya-śikṣāṣṭaka)* with the Bengali commentary of Manindranath Guha. Translated, introduced, and annotated by Neal Delmonico.

6. *Holy Name—Thought Jewel (Nāma-cintāmaṇi)* by Kānupriya Gosvāmī. In three volumes. Translated, introduced, and annotated by Neal Delmonico

7. *Mahāmantra (The Great Mantra)* by Sundarānanda Dāsa Vidyāvinoda. Translated, introduced, and annotated by Neal Delmonico.

8. *Moonlight on the Daily Acts of Kṛṣṇa*, the earliest meditation/visualization (*līlā-smaraṇa*) text of the Caitanya tradition, by Kavikarṇapūra. Translated, introduced, and annotated by Neal Delmonico.

www.ingramcontent.com/pod-product-compliance
Lightning Source LLC
Chambersburg PA
CBHW071203070526
44584CB00019B/2899
* 9 7 8 1 9 3 6 1 3 5 0 5 9 *